ON THE IDEA OF POTENCY

D1435068

ENCOUNTERS IN LAW AND PHILOSOPHY
SERIES EDITORS: Thanos Zartaloudis and Anton Schütz

This series interrogates, historically and theoretically, the encounters between philosophy and law. Each volume published takes a unique approach and challenges traditional approaches to law and philosophy.

General Advisor
Giorgio Agamben

Advisory Board
Oren Ben-Dor, *Law School, University of Southampton, UK*
Anne Bottomley, *Law School, University of Kent, UK*
Justin Clemens, *Faculty of Arts, University of Melbourne, Australia*
Emanuele Coccia, *École des Hautes Études en Sciences Sociales, France*
Jaś Elsner, *Corpus Christi College, Oxford, UK & Department of Art History, University of Chicago, USA*
Peter Goodrich, *Cardozo Law School, Yeshiva University, New York, USA*
Piyel Haldar, *Birkbeck College, Law School, University of London, UK*
Pierre Lochak, *Centre de Mathématiques de Jussieu, Université Paris 6 Pierre et Marie Curie, France*
Nathan Moore, *Law School, Birkbeck College, University of London, UK*
Alexander Murray, *English, University of Exeter, UK*
Clemens Pornschlegel, *Institut für Germanistik, Universität München, Germany*
Alain Pottage, *Law School, London School of Economics, UK*
Jacob Schmutz, *Department of Philosophy and Sociology, Paris-Sorbonne University, France*
Jessica Whyte, *School of Humanities and Communication Arts, University of Western Sydney, Australia*
Robert Young, *English, New York University, USA*

edinburghuniversitypress.com/series/enlp

ON THE IDEA OF POTENCY

Juridical and Theological Roots of the Western Cultural Tradition

Emanuele Castrucci

EDINBURGH
University Press

Edinburgh University Press is one of the leading university presses
in the UK. We publish academic books and journals in our selected
subject areas across the humanities and social sciences, combining
cutting-edge scholarship with high editorial and production values to
produce academic works of lasting importance. For more information
visit our website: edinburghuniversitypress.com

© Emanuele Castrucci, 2016

Edinburgh University Press Ltd
The Tun – Holyrood Road
12 (2f) Jackson's Entry
Edinburgh EH8 8PJ

Typeset in 11/13 Palatino by
Servis Filmsetting Ltd, Stockport, Cheshire,
and printed and bound in Great Britain by
CPI Group (UK) Ltd, Croydon CR0 4YY

A CIP record for this book is available from the British Library

ISBN 978 1 4744 1184 4 (hardback)
ISBN 978 1 4744 1185 1 (paperback)
ISBN 978 1 4744 1186 8 (webready PDF)
ISBN 978 1 4744 1187 5 (epub)

The right of Emanuele Castrucci to be identified as author of this work
has been asserted in accordance with the Copyright, Designs and
Patents Act 1988 and the Copyright and Related Rights Regulations
2003 (SI No. 2498).

Contents

Contents

For these latter persons seem to set up something beyond God, which does not depend on God, but which God in acting looks to as an exemplar, or which he aims at as a definite goal.
(Spinoza, *Eth.*, I, pr. 33, sch. 2)

It used to be said that God could create anything except what would be contrary to the laws of logic. The truth is that we could not say what an 'illogical' world would look like.
(Wittgenstein, *Tractatus logico-philosophicus*, 3.031)

to L.L.V.,
for what he has been

Preface

The studies gathered in this volume deal with the meta-physical concept of potency, considered in the sense that the modern philosophical lexicon since Spinoza (*potentia*) and Nietzsche (*Macht*) has in the main attributed to it. It is a very different concept from the original Greek *dynamis*, which Aristotle elaborated extensively in his *Metaphysics*. Actually, a radical critical reinterpretation of these texts – authentic sources of our Western philosophy – is certainly called for today.

The discussion that follows begins with the idea of the possibility that there exists an autonomous logic intrinsic to the metaphysical concept of potency, entirely immanent to it: a *logos* of potency which invests at the same time the theological dimension and the specifically theoretical dimension. To get to the crux of the matter: is there a *logos* capable of limiting the very power of God? This question places in strict relation an issue (the one about *logos*) that arises from classical Greek philosophy with the theological knowledge which originates from Jewish biblical exegesis. Two completely unrelated universes. Nevertheless, on a historical plane there indeed existed a link between these disparate areas, and it marked the destiny of the West. As Leo Strauss has masterfully shown, Christianity has constituted for millennia, among many contradictions, something like a juncture between two hitherto unrelated worlds: Greek philosophy and biblical revelation. And it has formed on this basis an entire civilisation: ours, which is now ending. It is therefore now even more fitting to consider the question of the «limits of God», specifically the logical rules which in some manner «limit» God's very action (or, more precisely, of that figure which incessant human mythopoeic activity has come to call 'God'), in the consideration that this question takes its cue from the profound need, before St Paul perhaps conceivable but in practice unworkable, of a relationship between these two extremely different worlds. Our West, with its grandiose but devastating philosophical rationalism, was born from this.

The first chapter of this volume therefore examines the hypothesis of a proto-rationalist Being «permeated by logos», and we immediately note a clash «at several removes» between two giants of modern philosophy, Leibniz and Spinoza. Their solutions to the metaphysical problem are radically divergent, yet equally representative of the highest level to which the issue can be raised. At the end of this chapter we make an explicit interpretive hypothesis – what might be called a 'neo-Spinozan' one – which underpins the entire system of this essay.

In the second chapter the problem is to examine how Spinoza's metaphysical apparatus relates to the philosophical tradition of the past, from Aristotle to the Arabic interpretations (first of all Averroes') of Aristotle's *Metaphysics*: namely the specific way in which Spinoza's ontology is opposed both to Greek-Arabic «necessitarism» and to the naive anthropomorphism of Jewish theology, derived from Revelation. The issue involves the ways in which the philosophy of law of the Western cultural tradition – from Augustine to Aquinas, and from Duns Scotus to Ockham – formulates the concepts of «natural law» and «natural right».

In the third chapter this problem is further investigated in its inner relationships, which concern the opposition between *potentia Dei absoluta* and *potentia Dei ordinata*, and the theoretical result reached is to point out, in direct disaccord with the canonic system of Aquinas's *Summa Theologica*, a substantial difference between the «jurisprudential model» of *potentia Dei absoluta* in Duns Scotus and the «logical model» of the same *potentia Dei absoluta* in William of Ockham.

This leads, in the fourth chapter, to a re-examination of the inherently problematic concept of a «political theology» mainly regarding the link between «creation *(ab aeterno)*» and «political constitution», the latter being considered in its profound ontological basis. We show how the Spinozan-Nietzschean hypothesis of «potency» cannot but exclude any modern form of «theological-political constitutionalism», namely any modern mode of limitation – largely determined by ethical motivations, or by the primacy of ethics over ontology: ethics of will over ontology of potency – of action exerted by potency itself. Here, we might say, Spinoza and Nietzsche come into play as a team against Kant and against all of Enlightenment natural law, revealing the weaknesses of the latter.

At this point another theorist joins the game: the German jurist and political theorist Carl Schmitt, who from the standpoint of an ultra-mature modernity interprets the array of forms inherited from classical metaphysics, allowing us today to establish an unexpected link between the ontological dimension of potency and the concept, juridical before political – and political in the strong sense – of «constituent power». The ways in which this concept, with its various theoretical issues, is reflected in our contemporary world – and precisely in our present historical period, which preludes the end of the West, understood as a horizon we have inhabited until now – is the subject of the last chapter of this essay, clarified by three illustrative corollaries: the first on the origins of modern conventionalist ethics, the second on the concept of political theology, the third on the rhetoric of ethical universalism in Jürgen Habermas. This is a finale short on hope but anchored in a solid, realistic analysis of what has become our contemporaneity.

E. C.

University of Siena, October 2015

I

The Logos of Potency:
A Theoretical Introduction

1. *A Being «permeated by logos». Substance-logos and function-logos.* – The symbolic image of logos stands traditionally to indicate the problem of an *intelligible means towards Being*: of an ultimate law ascribable to the structure of entities, framed by formal patterns of *representability*.[1] Is logos then a simple logical form of representation, fully inscribed in the ways of communicative human language? Or is it instead – as metaphysicians have often tended to suggest – something more: a substantial structure irreducible to the human intellect without loose ends? Platonists – as is known – have believed that the human intellect does not coincide with logos, even though it is a direct participant (*koinonía*) of logos, and thereby claim for this *substance-logos* the attribute of a solid metaphysical substance – one that contrasts with the fluidity of the idea of *function-logos*, of «logos as function», which predominates in the theory of modern contemporary science.

It is a fact that the latter idea of logos as function is indubitably predominant in the modern era. To say 'function-logos' means to see in logos nothing else and nothing more than the *general logical form of the human intellect*, an *operation* of the human intellect – therefore a form also capable of being reproduced artificially, under certain conditions of technological development. It seems thus that the image of a Being «permeated by logos», in which the gnosis of the «broader picture»[2] is reflected, could not – if framed in a modern epistemological context – but cease to refer to a solid holistic perspective determined by a single substance-logos, and be transformed into the theory

1

of a plurality of regional logoi, each of them illustrative of a single territory of Being, and each – hypothetically – unrelated to the others. But if the legitimacy of this change in perspective is recognised, what overall sense can the concept, no longer monistic but now pluralistic, of a Being «permeated» by unrelated logoi still have? Can it still support a gnosis (which either operates in terms of a unified vision or simply does not exist)?

2. Deus contra Deum? – These questions lead us at once too far afield and obviously do not yield a direct answer. For this reason it is more fitting for our purposes to start with another kind of question, namely: how was the Platonic-Christian (substantialist) idea of a Being «permeated by logos» made historically thinkable?

We know quite well, of course, how philosophical thought traditionally constructed, hand in hand with theological thought, the hypothesis of the *'self-subsistence' of an untransformable logical-ontological structure*, and how this route led to a cross-contamination between the attributes of logos and the attributes of God. However, on this point it behoves us to pause and survey some aporias.

In particular, it should be noted that in the reconstructions of traditional theology, inextricably linked to the creationist cosmological paradigm, two possible extremes were delineated, around which the thought of God came into play, but also faded out. Either the fundamental laws of Being were determined entirely by God's will, or – to some extent (as yet to be ascertained) – they pre-existed God. Voluntarism *versus* intellectualism. Obviously, only in the latter instance would there be room for an *autonomous* concept of logos, which would nevertheless, as a pre-existing essence, have ended up dangerously *breaking off from and clashing with* the divine essence. Then how can the leap from here to the radical heterodoxy of *Deus contra Deum* be avoided? How are we to think of the enormity of a God (still declared omnipotent) *subordinated to logos*? I think this is still today a powerful argument against the possibility of a philosophy of logos that would also call itself Christian: if logos has all the divine attributes (though with the exception of creative personality and causality), then logos becomes the *real God*; in short, Goethe's «*Nemo contra Deum nisi Deus ipse*» (*Dichtung und Wahrheit*, IV) continues to have validity.

The idea of a God-Logos 'diarchy' is a compromise whose unstable equilibrium lacks credibility. In fact, the «overarching vision» of the logos would be more convincing in a perspective that discarded creationism and rejected a personal God. What need is there, in fact, from the perspective of a desirable philosophical radicalism, for features of personality and a creator being as attributes of the primal substance? With Spinoza, for example, from the potency of an indifferent because impersonal God, coinciding with the totality of Being, all things were not created but «necessarily derived», and [would continue] forever by that very necessity: in the same way that «the nature of a triangle – from eternity and for eternity – is such that its three angles must be equal to two right angles» (*Eth.*, I, prop. 17, scholium).

I think, in a word, that it is necessary to make a choice: those who intend to think through the idea of a supreme and self-subsistent logos (supreme in that it is self-subsistent) must also be willing to give up, for obvious reasons of consistency, the idea of a personal God in his aspect of pure intellect, as delineated by the Christian theological tradition.[3]

3. *Aporias of Leibniz's solution.* – This choice was not made by the line of Platonic thought that through Leibniz flowed into modern idealism. This line maintained the concurrency of two spaces that, as sovereigns, were incompatible with one another: the space of logos as *a priori* condition of thinkability of the world (as a «logical construction» of the world), and the space of a personal Christian God. Just fifty years after Descartes' *Metaphysical Meditations*, Leibniz formulated the «principle of sufficient reason» that would serve as the core of his thought, consisting in the idea of

a «reason that is sufficient to determine why a thing is so and not otherwise». God was judged to be the source and extent of this reason, whose principles extended as a sort of natural logical law with regard to the totality of beings. And Leibniz, too, was referring to the personal Christian God, in his aspect of pure intellect rather than will.

In short, in Leibniz's eternal imprint, which is ever-present in any gnosis of Platonic-Christian intellectual inspiration, one must recognise a constant of thought, but also what, less benignly, could be considered as a coercion to think of logos as self-subsistent, or to conceive of real existence, in the world, of entities, objects, relations, that, insofar as they are traceable to truths of reason, are truly 'immutable' and cannot be other than what they are. In addition, followers of Leibniz, as always, when they claim the existence of truths whose reason is «*ipsa necessitas seu essentia*», do not intend so much to stop at the tautological cores of logical-mathematical truths of the type A = A, or 2 + 2 = 4, as to claim to penetrate, by an indiscriminate use of the criterion of analogy, into the realm of ethics, and of practical ethics in particular. Thus, in the mathematical-minded vision of the proponents of the natural law of logic (which bends the principle of analogy to its extreme consequences), «truths of reason» would also include the alleged principles of universal justice, seen as *a priori* conditions of any possible correct action.

4. *Spinoza vs Leibniz.* – However, these classical Leibniz-type responses, perfectly ensconced in the history of idealist metaphysics, appear to us unsatisfactory. Leibniz, as exemplar of the thought of his age, obviously cannot for an instant entertain the possibility that his «truths of reason», valid «in all possible worlds», are simply a *myth of logic*, or rather an idealist hypostatisation of the psychophysical mechanisms of the mind-brain compact. What clearly does not enter into Leibniz's field of vision is the possible nature of 'mental product' of the idea of logos: its nature of the typical conceptualisation of a particularly advanced

given phase of the natural history of the human species. A mental product, therefore, decidedly not universal if it is understood *sub specie aeternitatis*. The idea of logos should be relativised in the cosmic framework, since a thought that requires it is possible only in the presence of momentous conditions and of random but also unique forms of life in the development of Being.

The argument that one would therefore wish to oppose (Spinozically?) to the logocentric idealism *à la* Leibniz is that logos corresponds *to a specific level of the development of potency of the human intellect*: a level which implies the active determination (much more than the simple detection) of a *sequence of regularity* in the structure of entities. All this notwithstanding the constitutive impossibility, for logos, to *go beyond* the forms of representational thought, or beyond the coordinates offered to the human mind by just two attributes of humanly accessible Being: thought and extension.[4] It is worthwhile to note here in passing the greater cognitive productivity of Spinoza's schemas as compared with those of Leibniz: an aspect to which we will have occasion to return later.

5. *The «arcanum» of logos.* – In all probability, the true enigma of logos is that, at a certain point in the phylogenetic development of the human species, certain brain cells, so to speak, changed their primary function, closely linked to simple, elementary biological existence, and – at the pinnacle of a process involving a dizzying growth of complexity – developed higher mental functions, making possible an ever greater intelligibility of the physical world.

The conceptualisation of natural numbers is, according to Husserl, one of the crucial stages for attaining to the «logical construction of the world». A construction, however, that, as has been so far affirmed, seems unable to be understood in any other way: or referring to the unmodifiable, necessary structures of Being, whose intelligibility is already given *in re* according to the Platonic model, or – alternatively – in a purely conventional way, by recognising that it is only a matter of abstractions working *a posteriori* on real bodies/worlds.[5] *Tertium non datur*? In Spinoza (it is the hypothesis that will be considered in the conclusion of this essay) there is perhaps the embryo of a *tertium genus*.

6. *An interpretive hypothesis.* – A thematic category very different from the gnoseological one, but equally subject, in this sense, to the essentialism/conventionalism dilemma, is what we are interested in here, and what could be defined with some inevitable approximation as a *theological-political* area, indicating with that expression (and considering as obvious the reference to Schmitt's terminological usage),[6] in the first place, the phenomenon of the structural analogy subsisting between the figure of God as ontological sovereign, author of a *«fiat ens»*, and juridical-political sovereign, author of a *«fiat lex»*. Even in this field – related to practical action, as well as to its forms of final legitimacy on the basis of a transcendent 'truth' – the hypothesis of logos would pose serious cognitive problems. If we admit the existence of a logos coeval with God, a kind of *theological constitutionalism* would be established in the order of the world, with an ontological sovereign self-limited by (or self-limiting in) the impersonal structure of logos, analogous to the way a political sovereign limits himself before the impersonal structure of the law.

The purpose of the pages that follow is to verify the substantiality of such an 'objective measure' function exerted by logos in a theological-political context. In other words: is it really possible to «(re)discover, after theisms, contact with the great sapience of an Impersonal Law to which the gods themselves are subject»? Is it possible to see «placed beside God, before God, a rival if not an actual superior, who has all its attributes save personal ones and that of efficient creator causality, or the power to establish out of nothing (which would in any case be a nothing-of-substances, not a nothing-of-logos)»?[7] I believe that, in order to make complete sense of these crucial questions, not devoid, among other things, of prescriptive valences for human behaviour, it is necessary

6

first «to pass by way of description», namely to determine roughly the position of the problem with reference to some among its higher developments, discoverable mainly in medieval philosophy and theology (marked by the strong objections raised by the nominalist and voluntarist current against the metaphysical realism-essentialism current, as well as by the different interpretations of Aristotle), and further in the crucial relationship – which inaugurated the metaphysics of modernity – between Leibniz and Spinoza.

And, yet sooner, to assume an interpretive hypothesis. Our interpretive hypothesis lies in confronting the problem of the alleged objective nature of logos in the light of the metaphysical and theological phenomenon of *potency* (see also Chapters II and III). We will therefore discuss the existence – of great importance for the theological-political sphere – of a true *logos of potency*, in the dual sense of: *a*) an immanent logic to the movements of divine and human potency (related, that is, to both the classical problem of *omnipotentia Dei* and the immanent development of the physical and intellectual power of individuals, in the Spinozan sense); *b*) logos as ontological, normative limit to the intrinsic arbitrarism of potency, which by its nature is tendentially *absolute*. In the first instance 'logos potency' as a subjective genitive; in the second instance as an objective genitive. Our thesis is that only the use of the subjective genitive is theoretically admissible, since the other case is linked to a scarcely demonstrable substantialist conception of logos. It is not possible (as I will try to argue) to speak of «theological constitutionalism» because *potency has its own autonomous, immanent logic, not artificially delimitable by pre-constituted external entities*, as would be the case of the objective existence of a logos as ontological, normative measure. On the contrary, we will see, in the example of the *constituent power* drawn from political and juridical theory, the inexhaustible – and, in the Spinozan sense, undelimitable – nature of potency, as completion of, and at the same time superior in immanence to, the secularised theological tradition of *omnipotentia Dei* (see Chapter IV).

II

Logos of 'Potentia Dei'

1. *Potency and power. Spinoza's ethics of «potency of what is living».* – The basis of every theological-political problem is therefore, according to our hypothesis, the philosophical-theological concept of *potency* (*potentia*), in its structural and functional analogy with the juridical-political concept of *power* (*potestas*). Defining initially logos as

> the set of *a priori* conditions (mathematical, logical, ontological) of possibilities of manifestation, co-eternal with God, which God can neither produce nor abolish, and which would exist *etiamsi daremus non esse Deum*[1]

we immediately note that this definition of logos is likely to be reformulated as

> the ordering of God's potency in accordance with intelligible laws-rules-forms-ideas, co-eternal with God, which God cannot produce or abolish, and which would exist *etiamsi daremus non esse Deum*.

«Together with the *a priori* conditions of possibility of God's manifestation» and «the ordering of his potency in accordance with intelligible rules»: in both instances there is an attempt at a logical formalisation of Being, the former more theoretical, the latter explicitly theological, characterised by its reference to God's power-potency in his constitutive ordering.

In my opinion, these two possible definitions – and especially the latter – need to be compared with what can be considered the clearest, most significant standpoint on the matter in the tenets of modern natural law. I refer to the famous Chapter XVI of Spinoza's *Tractatus Theologico-Politicus*, namely the passage in which Spinoza argues as follows:

> Every individual has sovereign right to do all that he can; in other words [. . .] the rights of an individual extend to the utmost limits of his power as it has been conditioned. Now it is the sovereign law and right of nature that each individual should endeavour to preserve itself as it is, without regard to anything but itself; therefore this sovereign law and right belongs to every individual, namely, to exist and act according to its natural conditions. [. . .] Whatsoever an individual does by the laws of its nature it has a sovereign right to do, inasmuch as it acts as it was conditioned by nature, and cannot act otherwise. For instance, fishes are naturally conditioned for swimming, and the greater for devouring the less; therefore fishes enjoy the water, and the greater devour the less by sovereign natural right. [. . .] Wherefore among men, so long as they are considered as living under the way of nature, he who does not yet know reason, or who has not yet acquired the habit of virtue, acts solely according to the laws of his desire with as sovereign a right as he who orders his life entirely by the laws of reason. That is, as the wise man has sovereign right to do all that reason dictates, or to live according to the laws of reason, so also the ignorant and foolish man has sovereign right to do all that desire dictates, or to live according to the laws of desire.
>
> It follows from what we have said that the right and ordinance of nature, under which all men are born, and under which they mostly live, *only prohibits such things as no one desires, and no one can attain*: it does not forbid strife, nor hatred, nor anger, nor deceit, nor, indeed, any of the means suggested by desire. This we need not wonder at, for nature is not bounded by the laws of

human reason, which aims only at man's true benefit and preservation; her limits are infinitely wider, and have reference to *the eternal order of nature*, wherein man is but a speck; it is by the necessity of this alone that all individuals are conditioned for living and acting in a particular way. If anything, therefore, in nature seems to us ridiculous, absurd, or evil, it is because we only know in part, and are almost entirely ignorant *of the order and interdependence of nature as a whole*, and also because we want everything to be arranged according to the dictates of our human reason; in reality that which reason considers evil, is not evil in respect to the order and laws of nature as a whole, but only in respect to the laws of our reason.[2]

From this long passage it becomes clear that if there is a logos – seen as a metaphysical structure of a natural logical law – in this view of Spinoza's, it does not have so much to do with human reason, or with the conscious intentions of single individuals, as with what Spinoza calls the «eternal order of nature», or in other words, «the order and interdependence of nature *as a whole*». These concepts point to the existence of a broader *ratio* than the merely human one: an absolutely non-moralistic *ethic of what is living as such*, attentive exclusively to the phenomena of potency, which human beings who shirk serious philosophical examination are obliged to ignore.

Logos would then cease to oppose itself platonically, as transcendent reality, to the order regulated (as in the two previous definitions) and would become instead the immanent rule of the great dialectic between *reason* and *potency* of what is living: a reason and potency that are to be found only indirectly in the individual subject or collectivity of individual subjects, and instead located far from any anthropocentric logic, in the wholeness of Being. Herein – as has been convincingly noted – «lies Spinoza's true thought: above the *ductus* or *dictamen* or *lex rationis*, which from the standpoint of natural law is related to the limited sphere of human interest, there exists an *aeternus ordo* which extends to all of nature, of which man is just a *particula*, and by which the existence and behaviour of all, wise and foolish, are determined, each in its own way».[3] God and logos would thus be kindred by virtue of their common nature of conceptualisations of the highest stage of development of the potency of Being. 'Potency', and not 'having to be'. Thus every link between the idea of *logos* and the idea of *good* is broken: the philosophy (-theology) of logos is not in itself a philosophy (-theology) of good: 'good' becomes rather anything that has the potency to come into Being, and that as such is 'desired' by God.

Close attention should be paid to Spinoza's position, and especially to the fact that he does not believe in any *a priori* separate from the all-compact-Being, which has always been, and *coincides* with its own rules of formation, they too eternal. *Detaching these and opposing them to Being as logos is for Spinoza pure idealistic artifice.* We are here at the antipodes of every Leibnizian theodicy: logos, an empty logical form that describes the movements of Being and culls the *indifference of Being* to moralistic and anthropomorphic ethical criteria, allows us on closer inspection to make a connection between Spinoza and Nietzsche[4] and confirms the centrality of theological reflection in the process of formation of Western thought. The centrality of the theological dimension: because in the genealogy of Western knowledge there is the reflection on God (*theology*) that determines ontology and logic. Where we must take 'logic' in the broadest sense, bearing in mind that in fact some of its basic categories – such as those expressed in the antitheses between necessity and contingency, finite and infinite, etc. – are of typically theological derivation.[5]

2. «*Analogy of potency*». – The central thesis of every political theology is *that the theological problem of divine potency is constructed in such a way as to be a format for interpreting the 'secular' phenomenon of human potency: that the potency of God acts as a hermeneutic criterion in relation to the 'amount of*

power' expressed by the single individual (or collective subject) in the human world.

One could speak properly, in this case, of an «*analogy of potency*» between man and God, and the analogical criterion could also function in reverse: from man to God, so that the *same* rules – the same *laws* of movement of human potency – should apply (because of the ontological unity of Being, and with the exception of the finite/infinite proportion) to divine omnipotence, reconstructed by theological knowledge.

The relationship between God and Being is one of potency exactly in the sense that the personal God of Judeo-Christian theology exercises potency no less than wisdom already in the act of creation (*creatio ex nihilo*, as in *II Macc.* 7, 28). And here, in relation to the origins prior to Being, there are at least two basic possibilities, each alternative to the other: either the tendentially arbitraristic, philosophically 'non-ethical' Old Testament one, culminating in the Judeo-Christian concept of the omnipotence of God (the God of Israel), or the rationalist Greek one, which implies eternal *necessity of Being*, according to the classic twelfth book of Aristotle's *Metaphysics*, especially in the interpretation of Averroes and Siger of Brabant. We are familiar with the first possibility. Let us try to get a better idea of the second.

3. *The Aristotelian dynamis.* – In Aristotle's *Metaphysics* impersonal *dynamis* – a concept light years away from Old Testament «power» of God, and as such incommensurable with it – is the principle that determines the transition from non-being (*no-thing*) to entity: almost as if he wanted to complete an itinerary already undertaken by Plato in his famous definition of the *Sophist* (219b) «in all that from a preceding non-being is conducted to a successive being we say that the conducting is a producing (*poieîn*) and the being conducted is a being produced (*poieisthai*)», Aristotle too establishes a direct relationship between human potency and 'making', seeing in the latter the paradigm of every creation, understood as a «coming into being» of entities.

Dynamis then means the source, in general, of change or movement in another thing or in the same thing qua other, and also the source of a thing's being moved by another thing or by itself qua other. For in virtue of that principle, in virtue of which a patient suffers anything, we call it *capable of suffering*.[6]

Of special significance – we note – is the fact that in these contexts of philosophical analysis, Aristotle constantly relates the linguistic use of the words 'potency' and 'impotence' to that of 'possibility' and 'impossibility': what is 'possible' is what is 'potent' to come into being, 'potent' to happen. The term has an extension that covers all Being: every modification in the motion of entities is likely to be qualified in terms of *dynamis*, and this – Aristotle adds – in both a negative and a positive sense, because «for even that which perishes is thought to be 'capable' of perishing [. . .], for it would not have perished if it had not been capable of it; but, as a matter of fact, it has a certain disposition and cause and principle which fits it to suffer this».[7] In conclusion a bit further on: «sometimes it is thought to be of this sort because it has something, sometimes because it is deprived (*stéresis*) of something».

The analogy between potency and possibility mentioned in the fifth book is resumed and concluded in the ninth book:

From our discussion of the various senses of 'prior', it is clear that actuality is prior to *dynamis*. And I mean by *dynamis* not only that definite kind which is said to be a principle of change in another thing or in the thing itself regarded as other.[8]

The only limit to potency is logical impossibility or 'contradiction'. Only contradiction prevents the mere start of movement towards an act (*enérgeia*). Aristotle establishes by this an axiom which will be taken up frequently, even by Thomas Aquinas, in a theological context. «A thing is in a state of potency if the actualization of its declared potency implies no impossibility»: thus being seated and standing up at the same time, or the incommensurability of the diagonal of a square with the side.[9]

4. *Beaufret's hypothesis.* – 'Dynamis' is the categorical expression of the virtuality of the real, of 'being-able-to-be' prior to the coming into being of entities, and the concept finds here its semantic range. Being-able-to-be and being-able-to-do: there is an absolute neutrality in the categorical use of Aristotelian potency: a use which will disappear – or perhaps, as some interpreters believe, will be betrayed – in Thomistic theology, and – more generally – in the medieval Latin version of Aristotle, with the appearance of meanings allusive to 'force', or even to 'compulsion', non-existent in potency as *dynamis*. (*Dynamis* has nothing of *kratos* nor of *bía*.)

Moreover, according to Beaufret's stimulating claim, the classical notion of *dynamis* as *potentia* is found to be, at least indirectly, distorted by the misleading translation – also considered 'classical' – of *enérgeia* as the Latin *actus*. Beaufret's observation is worth quoting more fully:

[Such a translation] could not be more anti-Greek. It covers over the passage from one world to another, that is, the passage from the Greek to the Roman world, to which action is as essential as χάρις is to the former. [. . .] The word *force, vis* in Latin, is often used to translate the Greek δύναμις, which is, with ἐνέργεια, one of the fundamental terms of Aristotle's *Physics*. In this way Leibniz will be content, in supposedly going back to the Greek from the Latin, to situate in what he names τὸ δυναμικόν the very essence of what is with the argument that nothing *is* unless it is able to deploy force (*vis*). But *vis* is not the Greek τὸ δυναμικόν but rather βία [. . .].[10]

In this perspective Roman culture imposes itself, making force (*vis*), understood in turn as *potestas*, i.e. «power over», the very essence of what Lucretius called *natura rerum*, corresponding to the Greek *physis*. «From such a perspective», Beaufret goes on to say, «what we have to know about things is above all the "force and powers", *vis atque potestates* (*De Rerum Natura*, II), by which they act upon each other. We are at the antipodes here of any knowledge of φύσις according to ἐνέργεια and δύναμις [. . .]».[11] This is so because, from the perspective of the Greeks, concepts such as 'force' and 'efficiency' are never primary.[12] What counts is not the «play of forces», understood as external physical force or 'potent' constructions, but rather immanent *poieîn* presiding over the birth of the work: «The birth of the work is not for the Greeks a matter of force, but rather of what they named *knowing*», Beaufret concludes incisively.[13]

5. *Substantial differences in medieval interpretations of Aristotle.* – The fact is that medieval philosophy, in focusing on the theological problem in its Judeo-Christian 'creationist' version, will completely ignore this dimension of philosophical analysis about «knowing», and «wisdom». Medieval philosophy will eventually reconnect itself to Greek philosophy, but will do so by filtering it through the Roman mindset: only in this way can we comprehend the translation of *enérgeia* with *actus* and the subsequent Thomistic interpretation of the God of the Bible as *actus purus essendi*.[14] Beaufret recalls in this regard, in support of his thesis, the opinion of Heidegger, who in an essay writes: «What for Aristotle determines the entity in its being, or what describes how a given determination takes place, is a type of reflection that refers to a very different experience from that of the medieval doctrine of *ens qua ens*. But it would be foolish to maintain therefore that the theologians of the Middle Ages had *mis*understood Aristotle; they had rather understood *differently*, in conformity with another way of relating to Being».[15]

The medieval Christian perspective loses sight of the *impersonal necessitarism* governing the logic (and theology) of *aitíai*, replaced by the personality of the man-God, or the phenomenology of the 'creatural'. 'Potency' once again has as its model the *omnipotentia* of the Hebraic-Christian God, and not the *dynamis* in need of the God of the twelfth book of the *Metaphysics*, a supreme entity that Aristotle often significantly renders with the neutral *tò theîon*.

«From the perspective of Thomism» – it is still Beaufret speaking –

> there is nothing else in the world other than creatures – not for having phenomenologically encountered them as such, but *ex lumine divinae scientiae* [. . .] Before the verdant field Aristotle could still say: οὕτως ἔχει, 'it is so'. Enlightened by the Scriptures, Saint Thomas can only say: "This is the work of God the creator who, after having spoken to our fathers by the voice of the Prophets, came, in this end of time, to speak to us through his son, having established him as the inheritor of all things." Certainly, this is very well said, and Saint Thomas has every right to speak in this way following Saint Paul. What is peculiar, however, is that in doing this he turns to Aristotle for support. This, in addition, is not forbidden. But then it is no longer possible to shrink back from a debate with a more original interpretation of Aristotle's thinking than the one with which his apology for biblical creation could content itself. [16]

Beaufret obviously refers to the interpretation of the Arabs (Averroes at the top of the list), rediscovered in the Christian Middle Ages by such 'heretics' as Siger of Brabant.

6. *Greek-Arabic* «*necessitarism*» *and Hebraic anthropomorphic theology*. – In short, the Thomist interpretation of the entity as *actus essendi* or *actualitas*, despite authoritative dissenting voices like that of Gilson, does not correspond to a cognitive «progress»,[17] and does not even know the sober style that characterises the experience of the entity as simple presence. It corresponds instead to a heavy-handed metaphysical

attempt at a philosophical comprehension of the process of creation by interpreting it in analogy with the process of 'doing' (*agere*) traceable to a potent subject for whom creation becomes (*summa*) *actio*, or rather *unica actio solius Dei*. Here, too, '*actio*' anthropomorphically misrepresents Aristotelian *enérgeia*, which is not an action but rather an impersonal movement (a *kineîn*) from non-being to being.

Aristotle resolutely rejects the hypothesis that the *kineîn* is a *práttein*, a divine *agere*; and even *kineîn* does not resemble *poieîn*, which is a 'doing' in accordance with knowledge, to produce a work.[18] Of course, there is nothing in common with the Hebrew word *barâ'*, which designates the subjective, wilful character of the creation in the biblical text. The risk of anthropomorphism is markedly encountered in the latter instance (Spinoza will harp on this aspect),[19] but not in the case of *kineîn*, which does not lend itself to anthropomorphic theological elaborations. As for the ontology of the *actus* of the scholastics, it is already a ripe example of what Nietzsche called *Herabwürdigung Gottes*, or the demotion of God to an efficient *personal* cause (and as such no longer a neutral Aristotelian *aitía*, responding to an impersonal, non-willed logic of *necessity*).

Greek and Aristotelian *dynamis* is therefore quite a different concept from the Thomist and scholastic *potentia*, even though both have in the background the same logical problem. I am thinking, as already mentioned, of the problem of the overall mode of «being able to be» prior to «being», or the potency of the mind preceding 'reality'. In fact it is the potency of the human mind as «*possibility of being*» which forms the background of Aquinas's, Duns Scotus's and Ockham's interpretations of Aristotle, as it does those of Averroes and Siger. On the other hand, it is the potency of the mind – as Agamben notes – which is the hardest thing to conceptualise. An experience of potency as such is only possible

if the potentiality is thought of as *"potentiality not to"* (do or think something), if the writing tablet is able *not* to be written on. [. . .] The mind is therefore not a thing but a being of pure potentiality, and the image of the writing tablet on which nothing is written functions precisely to represent the mode in which pure potentiality exists. For Aristotle, all potentiality to be or do something is always also potential not to be or not to do (*dynamis mē einai, mē energein*), without which potentiality would always already have passed into actuality and would be indistinguishable from it. [. . .] The "potential not to" is the cardinal secret of the Aristotelian doctrine of potentiality, which transforms every potentiality in itself into an impotentiality (*Met.*, IX, 1, 1046, 32).[20]

7. *The fight against necessitarism.* – Conceiving the construction of Being as a logical network of 'potencies' and 'impotencies' aimed at creating the present system in the world means conceiving the great Aristotelian view of the world as a unique product of a single causal relationship. In other words, potency and act as cause and effect determine a universal framework of *regularity* and *necessity* which eliminates space for the intervention of a personal God. The world as a chain of immanent necessity, in which God himself (*tò theîon*) is an element of this necessity, is in the end another myth of origins, alternative to the Bible's *Genesis*. The history of Western philosophy and theology is marked by the reception of (and – not least – the strong reaction to) this logical construction of 'necessity'.

The strong appeal of the Judeo-Christian God present in the theology of the late thirteenth century has the explicit function of breaking this chain of necessity and mechanical Aristotelian potencies by reintroducing contingency and free will. In this sense, one must read the famous condemnation of 1277, of epochal significance, which Bishop Étienne Tempier of Paris, as theological authority, issued against «necessitarism».[21] After 1277, Christian theological orthodoxy stressed contingentism in a series of doctrines – more or less defined as nominalistic – on the primacy of will. (We note here that even some of the theses of a certainly non-suspect, yet too lukewarm, Thomas Aquinas merited an 'anti-necessitarian' condemnation that year.)

The emphatic voluntarism of Duns Scotus and Ockham (but their names are only the tips of a vast outcropping archipelago) can be interpreted in the light of the resurgence and renewed fortune of contingentism. A resurgence and hardly a start from scratch, because the same issues had already been raised in the Islamic world in the eleventh and twelfth centuries, during the dispute between the *falāsifa* and Sunni theologians (the *mutakallimun* or *loquentes*: 'talkers'). These supposedly inspired the original position of Al-Ghazali.[22]

Who moves – Al-Ghazali already wondered – the hand of the scribe to make it pass to the act of writing? According to what laws is the passage from the *possible* to the *real*? And if there is something like *possibility* or *potency*, what, inside or outside it, makes it 'come out' into existence? As Agamben argues in this regard, the *mutakallimun*, custodians of the pure Islamic faith and enemies of philosophy, «hold an opinion that not only destroys the very concepts of cause, law, and principle [i.e. any substantial form of logos, E. C.] but also invalidates all discourse on the possible and the necessary, thus undermining the very basis of the *falāsifa's* research. [They in fact] conceive of the act of creation as an incessant and instantaneous production of miraculous accidents that cannot influence each other and that are, therefore, independent of all laws and causal relations».[23]

The description of the a-causal (or anti-causal) potencies which determine the motion of bodies in this state of perpetual miracle anticipates much of what will become seventeenth-century occasionalism in Europe (I have in mind certain pages of Malebranche, which give us a glimpse of a Malebranche contra Descartes, as regards the exaltation of divine liberty).[24] So for Al-Ghazali,

the scribe moves his pen, it is thus not he who moves it; this movement is only an accident that God creates in the scribe's hand. God has established, as habit, that the movement of the hand coincides with that of the pen and that the movement of the pen coincides with the production of writing; but the hand has no causal influence whatsoever in the process, since an accident cannot act upon another accident [. . .]. For the movement of the pen, God thus created four accidents that do not in any way cause each other but merely coexist together. The first accident is my will to move my pen; the second is my potential to move it; the third is the very movement of my hand; the fourth, finally, is the movement of my pen. When man wants something and does it, this therefore means that, first, his will was created for him, then his faculty of acting, and, last of all, the action itself.[25]

8. *Potency and creation.* – It has been duly noted that «this is not simply a conception of the creative act that differs from the one offered by the philosophers. *What the theologians want is to break Aristotle's writing tablet forever, to drive all experience of possibility from the world.*»[26] What the medieval Islamic theologians advance against Aristotle and against the intellectual construction of the logos of entities as dialectic of possibility and reality, potency and necessity, is in fact a radical proposal that could be defined as the *delogicisation of the world*.

The essential point is that, in doing so, the problem of potency, excised from the human sphere, is simply transferred to the divine. God is no longer a cause (although supreme) among causes; he is no longer the *Summum ens* that the Aristotelian theology of the twelfth book of the *Metaphysics* described analytically, but is instead absolute will, whose potency is comparable to the *kratos* of the Biblical God: an immeasurable, omnipotent will that is not bound by any intelligible logos and that therefore dismisses the basis for any independent human potency. But a God so conceived, *without logos*, a God who could not want what he wants, «would be capable of wanting non-Being and evil, which is equivalent to introducing a principle of nihilism into God».[27] The unrestricted freedom of *God without logos* would contain, in other words, a principle of nihilism: a small stain of nothing that God himself could not avoid unless by renouncing a significant part of his own omnipotence. God must therefore 'restore to logos' his power, and theology recognise that the source of the intelligible order is not so much *in* God as *outside of* God, and only subsequently 're-introduced' into God when God *wills* (and he cannot avoid willing) the order he has meanwhile created. (A curious figure, that of a God reduced to carrying out rules originally alien to him.)

Theological propositions – of course – that scramble through the many difficulties of a rational thought applied to an infinite matter. Such as to often grant a glimpse of the abyss of a frank heterodoxy, or even the explicit declaration of the non-existence of God, if by the word 'God' we mean the God of doctrinal Christian orthodoxy.

A potency that 'wills' and that is limited by its own will, crystallised against it, which binds the potent subject to the law of a willed order: this is the mystery that seems constantly to escape rationalistic analysis. Every theology invariably subtends a mythology of potency.

9. *Two models of natural law.* – We have said: the great difficulties of rational thought applied to an infinite subject matter. Herein lies the problem of natural theology, understood as the place where a definition is made, in the light of a human reasonableness often bordering on common sense, of the relationship between the acts of a creator God and a supposed system of substance-ideas, coexistent with God and therefore describable in the context of the theological imagination as «God's thoughts».

Hans Welzel, in his masterly work on *Naturrecht und materiale Gerechtigkeit*,[28] makes a clear distinction within the theology of philosophers between what he calls the idealist-intellectualist line of tendency and the voluntaristic-existentialist line of tendency. The first, represented by Plato and Thomas Aquinas (and later by

Leibniz), would give maximum space and maximum value to natural theology, understood as an investigation of a system of *ideas* and intelligible *laws*, on an equal footing with God. The second, represented by Augustine and the Franciscan school of Duns Scotus and Ockham, would do its utmost to uphold the positivity of Scripture: the theological *positum* of revelation, by an unequivocal subordination of human knowledge to the central idea of divine omnipotence. On the one hand, natural theology, with its exaltation of the role of ideas as epiphanies of logos; and on the other, theological voluntarism, revolving around the idea of God as the only necessary substance, which he wields at will on a horizon of total contingency, in the absence of 'necessary' laws of formation and development of entities.

10. *System of substance-ideas and personal God.* – The relationship between *system of substance-ideas and personal God* is inherently conflictual: it is indeed, we might say, conflict itself, 'proto-conflict'. One should wonder in this regard: in what way are ideas a limitation of the divine essence? Or, more precisely, with Welzel: are ideas such as «eternal essences in the mind of God»[29] *an integral part of the divine essence* or external to it? Aquinas's intellectualism cannot but respond in the first sense: «*idea Deo nihil aliud est quam Dei essentia*»,[30] seeking thereby to defuse the conflict. But the voluntarist Duns Scotus does not accept such an opinion: Scotus (and with him Ockham) was moved to this by what Welzel calls «the effort to degrade ideas, whose existence he could not deny, with respect to the essence of God, and to subordinate them to it».[31] If a presence of logos, according to Scotus, can still be recognised in the prohibition of logical contradiction and the existence of certain impossibilities «even for God» (for example, it is impossible that, given this system of reality, the sum of two right angles is not 180°), this presence, significantly, *is no longer detectable among the norms of practical action, namely with regard to the entire domain of ethics,* and this because – as Scotus himself claims in a drastic way in

a famous passage of his work – «the universal laws of correct action are established by the *will* of God, and not by his *intellect* [. . .], for in those laws there is to be found no conceptual necessity (*"quia non invenitur in illis legibus necessitas ex terminis"*)».[32, 33]

Above all – Welzel insists – Scotus no longer knows the Aristotelian-Thomistic doctrine of the *substantial nature of things*: the *'perseitas'* described in the *Summa Theologica* (I, qu. 63, 1 to 4), destined to provide the basis for the precepts of natural law. To the point of concluding:

> The natural law tradition of Aristotelian-Stoic origin (*orthós logos*), until then prevailing, is thus deprived of its fundamental thesis. 'Conformity to nature' serves as its basis for determining the content of the precepts of natural law. *The 'nature' of man conferred a material content to natural law.* Aquinas' theory, that there was a correspondence between the order of natural *inclinations* and the order of natural *rules*, moved entirely in this traditional framework. This natural law 'bridge' from the nature of man to the norm is now broken. The content of natural law *proceeds from on high, from God, not from below, from nature,* not even if this is understood as the essential form of man.[34]

11. *Summary.* – In brief, it is clear from what has been said that not even medieval Christian theology experienced a sufficiently homogeneous elaboration of the theme of *logos as autonomous reality*, in some way 'different from God'. In denying, generally, autonomy to this concept, Christian theology showed itself much more akin to the Old Testament model than to the idealist Greek model, to which Thomism seems to turn more directly (and hence contradictorily). In any case, Christian theology, with its indelible residue of anthropomorphism, leaves the way open for a theological-political elaboration, or for what we previously called the «analogy of potency» between creator and creature, which we must now determine more

accurately. It is therefore fitting to start from here in order to take on at closer quarters, in connection with authors such as Aquinas (§ 2), Duns Scotus (§ 3) and Ockham (§ 4), the controversial issue of *omnipotentia Dei*, where the idea of logos appears as an inherent limitation, and as such is constantly neutralised by theologians.

III

'Potentia Ordinata' *vs* 'Potentia Absoluta'

The purpose [of Scripture] is not to teach a science [. . .]; it does not demand from men other than obedience, and condemns only disobedience, not ignorance.

(Spinoza, *TTP*, XIII)

1. *Ontology of potency against ethics of will.* – «God's choice», which creationist theology speaks of, corresponds to what on the philosophical plane is the constitution of Being as contingency on the part of the only necessary substance, in which – as Scholasticism repeats – 'essence' and 'existence' coincide. Only this personification of God as original *constitutive force* makes possible – as we shall see later – a political-theological development, elaborated as an analogy of Being and yoking together under the same law the motions of divine potency and human potencies. In this sense, the effect is produced of nullifying the incommensurability of divine potency, lowering it to the modest commensurability of actions originating from an *entity*, no different in its essence (although qualified as «supreme») by other entities. This has the further result of authorising the application to God of fundamental metaphysical distinctions that characterise the common nature of entities, such as those between will and intellect, essence and existence, etc.

In other words: in Western theological ethics God is anthropomorphised so that we can speak of God, and everywhere the ontology of divine potency is reduced to ethics of intellect and will, when not to a dialectic of a misunderstood freedom in the realm of values. But the ontology of potency is far superior to the ethics of a will deemed free because, as it is assumed, capable of choosing sovereignly among values! Here we have Spinoza against (in the best hypothesis) Kant. We again refer to Agamben's observations on this point:

> Our ethical tradition has too often sought to circumvent the problem of potency by reducing it to the terms of will and necessity: not what you *can*, but what you *will* or *must* is its predominant theme [. . .]. But potency is not will and impotence is not necessity: believing *that will has power over potency*, that the transition to the act is the result of a decision that puts an end to the ambiguity of potency (which is always power to do and not do) – this is precisely the perpetual illusion of morality.[1]

A radical criticism must be levelled against that «oblivion of potency» that the Western secular ethics has unknowingly inherited from anthropomorphic theology. Potency cannot be reduced to a «fact of will», but instead possesses its own independent articulation, its own logic, which it is the task of philosophical thought to decipher.

2. *The misunderstandings of Aquinas.* – In Thomas Aquinas there occurs in this connection, inspired by a normalising intent, the most conscious misunderstanding of the logic of potency, forcibly translated in terms of a logic of will (and thus of intellect, since «will is intimately connected with intellect»).[2]

In the very Question 19 of the first part of the *Summa*, which deals with the problem of God's 'will', this notion is interpreted significantly as a mere desire, common to all entities and especially present in the supreme entity, to «have others participate as much as possible in their own good»:

> For natural things have a natural inclination not only towards their own proper good, to acquire it if not possessed, and, if possessed, to rest therein; but also to

spread abroad their own good amongst others, so far as possible. Hence we see that every agent, in so far as it is perfect and in act, produces its like. *It pertains, therefore, to the nature of the will to communicate as far as possible to others the good possessed*; and especially does this pertain to the divine will, from which all perfection is derived in some kind of likeness. Hence, *if natural things, in so far as they are perfect, communicate their good to others, much more does it appertain to the divine will to communicate by likeness its own good to others as much as possible.*[3]

In this text, divine will appears already conceptually predetermined by its link with good, and potency is reduced to mere 'executory' power of will, as Aquinas states more clearly in another context.[4] For Aquinas, God is omnipotent because wherever his power does not extend (*e.g.* «God cannot arrange things in such a way that affirmation and negation are both true together»), it follows that he has not willed it to be extended:

Accordingly there are three ways in which it is said to be impossible for a thing to be done. First, by reason of a defect in the active power, whether in transforming matter, or in any other way. Secondly, by reason of a resistant or an obstacle. Thirdly, because that which is said to be impossible cannot be the term of an action. *Those things, then, which are impossible to nature in the first or second way are possible to God.* [. . .] Consequently he cannot make yes and no to be true at the same time, nor any of those things which involve such an impossibility. Nor is he said to be unable to do these things through lack of power, but through lack of possibility, such things being intrinsically impossible: and this is what is meant by those who say that *'God can do it, but it cannot be done'.*[5]

Anyone will take a dim view of this double-talk, these word-games which make the same thing simultaneously possible *a parte Dei* and impossible *a parte obiecti*. What is clear is the embarrassment of admitting the secret of the *limit* that God's power encounters in 'not being able' to modify the logical order chosen and created by God himself, and that ergo is seen as co-eternal with God. Certainly the 'co-eternity' with God of logical structures belonging to a Being 'created' by God himself is a mystery: a reality not as such capable of being expressed in satisfactory analytical terms. To resolve the issue, Aquinas does not hesitate to resort to Augustine's problematic distinction, which tends to logically separate a «temporal beginning» from a «beginning of the foundation» of creation:

> [. . .] a beginning, not of time, but of cause. 'For as if a foot', they say, 'had been always from eternity in dust, there would always have been a print underneath it; and yet no one would doubt that this print was made by the pressure of the foot, nor that, though the one was made by the other, neither was prior to the other; so,' they say, 'the world and the gods created in it have always been, their Creator always existing, and yet they were made.'[6]

Concluding with:

> Therefore God could *make* something *that always was.* God can do in the creature *whatever is not inconsistent with the notion of a created thing*: else he were not omnipotent.[7]

But is the «notion of a created thing» in this last passage – the ontology of created condition – then also an 'immutable' condition for God? If that is so, how can it be compatible with the idea of divine omnipotence? Neither Augustine nor Aquinas responds convincingly on this point. Certainly, God would deny himself if he violated the order of justice willed by himself, which had therefore become 'his' justice; and on the other hand it is also true that omnipotence does not signify power to carry out *all* actions and to choose among *all* orders of reality, since many actions and many orders are marked by imperfection, expressive of a *defectum potentiae*, and are therefore not referable to God.[8] But even apart from the hypothesis of a 'bogus power' (namely, designating an activity involving the imperfection of the agent), the problem of the logical limits of an ordering action has in itself far-reaching philosophical implications. Despite the magnitude of the problem, Aquinas limits himself to summarising his argument in the following way:

> And as regards things that imply a contradiction, they are impossible to God as being *impossible in themselves*. Consequently God's power extends to things that are possible in themselves: and such are the things that do not involve a contradiction. Therefore it is evident that God is called almighty because he can do all things that are possible in themselves.[9]

Here Aquinas skirts the elementary fact that if God is truly almighty, the very notion of 'impossibility' vanishes, and *any* logical order is prone to be subject at any time to a sovereign 'revocation'. But it must be considered that even in this hypothesis God's potency tends now to be transformed from *absolute* (i.e. linked to a punctually 'miraculous' event) to *ordained*. This because an exception willed by God in the face of the logical-ontological order in force – chosen by God – rather than signifying a simple disavowal of it, causes its *extension* into a broader paradigm, not contradictory to the first, but such as to incorporate it into a new 'normality'. (But in Aquinas there is of course no trace of this problem, which emerges instead, as we shall see, in Duns Scotus.)

3. *Definitions of «potentia absoluta». The 'jurisprudential' model of «potentia absoluta» in Duns Scotus.* – Aquinas can reach his own conciliatory, 'normalising' conclusions

only as long as he avoids delving further into the aporias that accompany the *logic of a sovereign subject*, or – to state it better – as long as he avoids systematising the «state of exception» that always qualifies the sovereign choice for an order. (Carl Schmitt's *Politische Theologie* will provide the interpretive key of this process.)

It is in this direction that the concept, deliberately devalued in Aquinas's economy of thought, of God's *«absolute potency»* (*«potentia Dei absoluta»*), in its logical opposition to the *«potentia Dei ordinata»*, comes into view. Obviously it is the voluntarist theologians, incredulous about the ontological proportions of natural reason as a human-divine go-between guaranteed by the analogy of Being, who are the primary exponents of this distinction. It is worth dwelling on this point, on which – as we shall see – numerous possibilities for theological-political development will depend.

We note at once that the subject refers to a prevalently medieval literature which, though vast, is not always up to recognising the philosophical significance of the actual problem.[10] Among the first theologians to state the distinction squarely is Peter of Tarentaise (the future Pope Innocent V), who, commenting between 1256 and 1258 on Peter Lombard's *Sentences*, expresses himself in these terms:

> There is an order simply understood (*ordo simpliciter*) and there is an order that corresponds to the world as it is now (*ordo ut nunc*): in the first sense [God] can *by means of absolute potency*; in the second sense he can *by means of ordained potency*. [. . .] It follows that [God] by means of absolute potency can accomplish what he cannot by means of ordained potency, since many things, though not part of the world order as it is now, are nevertheless subject to his potency.[11]

In this first doctrinal discussion of the question *«an Deus possit aliqua de potentia absoluta, quae non potest de potentia ordinaria»*, the two types of potency differ from one another in relation to the fundamental dichotomy *ordo simpliciter/ordo ut nunc*. The order of divine potency as such is absolute, *ordo simpliciter*: simple potency in its constituent absoluteness, free as such of 'constituted' rules logically subsequent to it. With the proviso, however, that the ordering of Being chosen by God *ut nunc*, in its elaboration of secondary causes linked among themselves, possesses its own relative *de facto* autonomy: an autonomy that makes it possible to reserve parenthetically, *ut nunc*, the possibility of an extraordinary intervention by God *de potentia absoluta*, such as to revocate in its exceptionality the order established up to that moment as the only existing one.

It is not a matter of two different potencies, but only of two different modes of the same potency referable to God. On this point theological doctrine is unanimous in considering absolute potency as a potency in turn ordained, but ordained – as already stated – according to a different, broader order than the one existing *ut nunc*. The most significant text illustrating this point is the famous passage in Duns Scotus's *Commentary* on Peter Lombard's *Sentences* (*Ox.*, I, dist. 44, *single qu.*). Note that on the two canonical definitions of the distinction between *potentia ordinata* and *potentia absoluta* – Scotus's and Ockham's – there is no agreement, but on the contrary – as has been convincingly demonstrated[12] – there is a clear-cut opposition which demands closer examination.

Hence Scotus: «Jurists say that those who can do [something] *de facto*, do so by their inherent power; those who can do [something] by law, do so by ordained power according to pre-existing rules.»[13]

It is clear that the intention of Scotus's text is to bring action (divine, but not only divine) *de potentia absoluta* into the realm of *de facto* possibilities and, as a corollary, *de potentia ordinata* action into the realm of *de jure* possibilities. Absolute potency and ordained potency are thus configurable as two circles of different diameter, the first of which contains the second. This means that each actor is attributed the right to choose freely whether to act *de jure*, according to a fixed rule, or to act *de facto*, as an exception to this rule, according to an absolute potency that virtually brings about a new order:

> In every subject acting by intellect and will, capable of acting in accordance with just law, yet in such a way as not necessarily to act in accordance with it, we can distinguish between an ordained potency and an absolute potency. The reason for this is that this subject can act in accordance with that just law, and then acts according to ordained potency (ordained, in fact, as the beginning of execution of the just law), but can also act outside of the law or against it, and this is absolute potency, which surpasses ordained potency.[14]

And again:

> When in the potency of the agent are to be found both the law and the criteria for the determination of its justice, so that no law can be said to be just unless it was requested by said subject, then the latter can act righteously by acting in a way that differs from the disposition of that law, since he can always consider just another law, according to which he will act in an ordained manner. Nor then will it be said that his absolute potency simply surpasses the ordained potency, since the action will still be considered ordained with respect to this other law.[15]

It seems clear that Scotus's interpretive model is essentially of a theological-political nature, in the sense that it is able to pave the way for productive analogies in the use of the concept of *potentia absoluta* on the part of the jurisprudence of the political power. Scotus, in particular, in maintaining that we are dealing with absolute power whenever the subject agent (God or man) is free to act outside of the given order, seems to usher in what might be called the principle of free 'jurisprudential' manipulability of the logos that presides over any given normative order. This has the fundamental consequence of making applicable *new* criteria of justice, which impose themselves then as elements expressive of a *new ordained potency*. As has been incisively noted, «God is not obliged to introduce gravitation into creation, since the proposition "there exists a world without gravity" implies no contradiction [. . .]. An occasional suspension of the law of gravity (a "miracle") would be understood as belonging to the plane of *potentia ordinata*, and in fact it would have been *ab aeterno* foreseen and foreordained.»[16]

Scotus never tires of insisting on this point, and there are numerous passages in his works in which he elaborates on this concept:

[God], as he can act in exception of a law, could thus establish any other law as just. If this were established by God, it would certainly be just, since no law is just if not explicitly established by God's will. [The action] would not be ordained according to the first criterion of order, but according to a different order which divine will always has the faculty to impose.[17]

In other words, any act of God, as well as that of any other freely acting subject, can always be interpreted as an expression of *ordained* potency. If the agent is free will («*quando lex est in potestate agentis*»), its action can *always* be made to fall under a rule (*lex*) in respect of which it can be considered *de potentia ordinata*.

Juridical methodology (a key part of the philosophy of law) teaches us to analyze the mechanisms of implementation of an order – established as the overall *finality* – in a particular action (a single *factum*), and it constitutes in this sense a secularised version of the theological hermeneutics of potency. At the base of both there is the presence and decisive function of a *juridical (or 'jurisprudential') logos*, proceeding according to the principle that every action *de potestate absoluta,* interpreted differently, is prone to appear as *de potestate ordinata.* The crucial point is that in the pure voluntaristic hypothesis, lacking an objective framework of legality as a previously established standard of reference, *any* act of a sovereign power which seems to constitute (*de facto*) a violation of the given order, will create implicitly (*de jure*) a new order, a new general rule (in epistemology we would say: a new *paradigm*), in light of which the action will not be considered an exception or a violation, but a particular instance of application in an expanded order, up to then invisible. (This consideration too prevents – already at first glance – the existence of a logos as objective criterion in the practical sphere.[18])

4. *The 'logical' model of* «potentia absoluta» *in Ockham. Courtenay's thesis.* – If Duns Scotus is, as we have said so far, the author who makes the first real use of the theological-political idea of absolute potency, Ockham is the author who most successfully perfects the *logical* model of the world as contingency, building what Gilson efficaciously defines as a «radical contingency of finite being».[19]

Ockham is the anti-Aristotle (or, should we say, the anti-Averroes): he substitutes the Greek-Arabic postulate «all things are necessarily caused» with the equally clear counter-postulate «all things are contingency put in place by a personal God», expressive of the absolute freedom of the creator in relation not only to creation, but to some extent also to uncreated logos[20]. But how can contingency be defined in terms of modal logic, that is, the modality of the absolute *freedom* of divine action, to counterbalance the *necessity* of logos? Leibniz, in his *Elements of Natural Law,* sums up the classical logical modalities:

The fourth figure is, precisely, contingency, which he defines as «*quicquid potest non fieri*», or the metaphysical space of free action.

In looking at this scheme, one inevitably notes with Agamben the difficulties that characterise, precisely on the metaphysical plane, the thought of contingency:

possibile		potest	
impossibile	est quicquid	non potest	fieri
necessarium		non potest non	(seu verum esse)
contingens		potest non	

If Being at all times and places preserved its potential not to be, the past itself could in some sense be called into question, and moreover, no possibility would ever pass into actuality or remain in actuality [i.e. would always remain under the threat of what in theological-political language is a *sovereign revocation!*, E. C.]. The aporias of contingency are, as a result, traditionally tempered by two principles.

The first, which could be defined as the *principle of the irrevocability of the past* (or of the unrealisability of potentiality in the past) [...] is the principle that the Latins expressed in the formula *factum infectum fieri nequit*, and that Aristotle, in *De coelo*, restates in terms of an impossibility of realising the potentiality of the past: 'there is not potentiality of what was, but only of Being and Becoming'.

The second principle, which is closely tied to the first, is that of conditioned necessity, which limits the force of contingency with respect to actuality. Aristotle expresses it as follows: 'what is is necessary as long as it is, and what is not is necessary as long as it is not' (*De interpretatione*, 19a, 22).[21]

What Ockham seems to have in mind is something very close to this Aristotelian principle of «conditioned necessity», when in a passage of his *Tractatus contra Benedictum* he appears to impose a fundamental limit to the logic of God's absolute potency, observing that God *in fact* will never act on the basis of it (*de facto numquam faciet*).[22] Perfect contingency qualifies – we said – the moment preceding the divine decision for a logical order, and does not involve the possibility of exceptions to that order once it has been chosen by God: considering God's action as *de potentia absoluta* means reasoning «on possible worlds, not on God's possible subversive intervention in this world».[23] The matter does not hinge upon 'miracles', but on the logic of possible worlds.

The Ockham text to examine in this regard is *Quodlibet* VI, where Ockham states the following:

> The distinction [between *potentia ordinata* and *potentia absoluta*] must not be understood as if in God there were really two different potencies [. . .] because God cannot do anything outside of an order (*nihil potest facere inordinate*). But it must be understood in the sense that sometimes 'power to do something' refers to laws ordained and established by God, and then it is said that God can act by ordained potency. Sometimes instead 'power means *being able to do what does not imply contradiction*, whether God has ordained it or he has not ordained it'.[24]

Ockham's very theory of the production of entities as absolute contingency therefore encounters a core of logos which to some extent redimensions its scope: God cannot interfere arbitrarily with Being because «*Deus potest facere omne quod fieri non implicat contradictionem*». Here the theology of omnipotence seems to clash with the ontology of the thing created, which gives forth its own logic, about which not even God can make an exception. This is because it is true that in God there is the capacity, the active potential to make choices which, however, he does not want to make, which he has never made, nor will ever make, but *God cannot weaken himself* by placing in being a potency that betrays an impotence. And in any case he does not act out of necessity: he could make things different, build different orders from the ones he has decided to make/build.

Hence it is theologically correct, for Ockham as for Aquinas, to maintain that the order established by God is not identical to the order of his goodness, justice and wisdom, for the goodness, justice and wisdom of God could have been expressed (and more intensely) in another system. In any case it must be considered – and this point deserves close attention – that the 'limit' set on God's choice derives from the *pactum*, the *covenant* which lies at the origin of the ontological order chosen by God with the creation.

Courtenay, more than any other scholar, has carried out an in-depth analysis (relative to Ockham, but extend-able to virtually all late-medieval thought) of the major issues in this direction. The *pactum* or covenant at the origin of *this* order of Being is the great decision that freely expresses the nature of God. God (and on this point all theologians are by professional definition anti-Aristotelian, anti-Averroist and, obviously, anti-Spinozan) *is not subject to necessity*, and therefore *could have chosen* a different order, decided upon a different ontology and a different logic. But his choice, configured as dialogical with respect to the Being created, biblically constitutive of an alliance, determined in the Being created a sort of legitimate expectation and confidence in the realisation of the logical order chosen. The Cartesian *trompeur* God is here radically excluded. [25] Here the nature determined by that initial pact is a minimal form of logos, so that one may think with Courtenay of a sort of «contractual rela-tionship» between God and man, to which a foundational character is attributed.

I quote from Courtenay:

It was not the atomistic metaphysics of the individual (so long misunderstood) nor the epistemology of intui-tive cognition (Scotist in origin and adopted by almost everyone in the late Middle Ages) that distinguished this movement [i.e. Ockhamism], but rather a conception of *centrality, efficacy, and dependability of verbal, contractual agreements for all aspects of the relationship between God and man*. Each individual idea in this moderate nominalist system (for example, the idea of the two powers of God, or the semi-Pelagian soteriology, or the non-necessity of the Judeo-Christian ethical system, or the idea of *sine qua non* causality in the sacraments) can probably be found in earlier thinkers or in contemporaries to whom one would never apply the terms nominalist or Ockhamist. The unique feature of Ockhamist thought was that these ideas were all present and grounded in the *idea of pact, or covenant – willed verbal agreements that are no less dependable and certain because they are in origin voluntary.*[26]

The role attributed to the Old Testament concept of God is therefore central to this line of reasoning: a God who – so Courtenay says – «remains omnipotent and free, and who communicates directly with man through covenants». Courtenay's considerations are intriguing and deserve attention in their ability to highlight the link between Ockhamism and conventionalist epistemology, no less than to show the role Ockham played in combating the realist ethical naturalism that had formed the standard view of medieval theological reflection.[27]

It seems to me that Courtenay's view converges substantially with Villey's concerning the possible consequences in the juridical-political sphere of this epistemological approach:

In the end nominalism also influences the sphere of law [. . .] Natural law has lost all its universal, compulsory authority, at least as regards the legislator. Indeed, the conclusions that jurists draw from the laws [. . .] can have validity only for the duration of the legislative will that served as their foundation: *nisi statuatur contrario.* The legislative authority that founded the system of property ownership is perfectly justified in establishing that, in some cases, a deposit need not be returned; or [. . .] the Christ who founded the Church could have established that the Pope is not the successor of Peter or the bishop of Rome.[28]

What matters is the force of authority which imposes the convention. If this force is sufficient, then it can reasonably be assumed that the *order* (both logical and juridical) that issues from it will be *stable*, unthreatened by 'exceptions' or 'miraculous' acts that could perilously subvert the paradigm. It will therefore act as a good substitute for the principles of a universal logos.

IV

Political Theology Reconsidered

1. *A pattern of correspondences.* – Logic of substitution, transfer and secularisation of theological patterns in the immanence of politics: as far back as the late Middle Ages these mechanisms were consolidated into a new epistemological framework, which would entrench itself in an odd fashion in the modern age. Hence the modern age would not take shape as a clear-cut alternative to the classical forms of theological thought, but (contrary to Blumenberg's hypothesis of «absolute metaphor»)[1] would continue to utilise the patterns of theology by retracing them continually anew through the powerful principle of analogy.

We must begin with what can be defined as the «primary analogy», or the presence of the structural homologue between theology and jurisprudence, already noted by Leibniz.[2] Many inferences may arise, and have in fact arisen in this regard, from Schmitt's outburst, «Alle prägnanten Begriffe der modernen Staatslehre sind säkularisierte theologische Begriffe»:[3] theology and jurisprudence are guided by the same «duplex principium» of *scriptura* and *ratio* as described by Leibniz, or by the close relationship that develops between a corpus of dogmatic truths contained in a written text (endowed therefore with a sacred aura of potent intensity) and a hermeneutic apparatus designed to attribute meaning to the tenets of the *Veritas scripta*. The analogy appears at once in its most typical form in the relationship between Holy Writ, «liber authenticus», in which the theological *positum* concerns the dominance of an almighty God over the world, and positive law, in which the objective of hermeneutic activity is the dominance of the sovereign over human society. God and Nature in the first case, the State and law in the second.

Already Kelsen, in an essay published in the same year as Schmitt's *Politische Theologie*, drew attention to the same thematic nodes, with the intention of demythologising/demystifying what he called «the pseudo-problem of the relationship between a system and its hypostatisation».[4] He concluded: «If one interprets the sovereignty of the State as potency, this is precisely the potency that any theology claims as the essence of God, and that, elevated to absolute omnipotence, is also claimed by the State.»[5]

It is certainly not fitting here to examine in depth the peculiarities of Kelsen's critique, aimed, as is known, at reaffirming the normativistic identity of the State and law against any ontological hypostasis. It suffices to note how this attention – already widespread in the juridical doctrine of the early decades of the twentieth century – to what we called «primary analogy» (God's transcendence and transcendence of power) spawns a number of significant correspondences. Among them:

(*a*) 'Creation' of an order of Being by one almighty God.

First hypothesis: God creates everything except logos, which has 'always been' *in mente Dei*: it is the thought of God not created by God because 'co-essential' to God. First a Thomist hypothesis, then a Leibnizian one (see point *c*). The result: *theological constitutionalism*, or objective (i.e. ontological, non-voluntary) limitation of God in logos. Limitation whose proper 'science' lies in natural rational theology, which then becomes a kind of human mirroring of God's knowledge.

Second hypothesis: God creates, together with the world, a system of ideas and essences, which, however, could have 'been otherwise' if God had so wished. Here we have *theological voluntarism*, or full freedom of divine decision about (and about the modifiability of) the logical-ontological constitution of Being, declared inaccessible to natural theology (which appears totally devalued) and more generally to any effort of human reason. (Therefore an opening onto a fideistic, *theistic*, non-deistic perspective.) Here logos is exclusively *in mente Dei*, and counts as creatural essence, even if it remains forever – as in the previous hypothesis – a prescriptive-normative essence.[6] (This is the case of the *potentia Dei absoluta* in the Scotus-Ockham doctrine, but also – and perhaps more forcefully, in the 'modernist' perspective – of Cartesian theology: see further, § 2.)

(*a'*) 'Foundation' of a political order by a sovereign power.

First hypothesis: *political constitutionalism*, or self-limitation of the constitutional monarch in the positive constitution. This self-limitation rests on an ontological base (and not merely a voluntary one, as in the model of the positivist juridical *Selbstverbindung*). Primacy of the law (as impersonal ontological structure rooted in rationality) over the legislator. Bracton (thirteenth century): «lex facit regem». Nineteenth-century parliamentary monarchy: «le roi règne mais il ne gouverne pas» (Thiers). Liberal constitutionalism.

Second hypothesis: *political voluntarism*, or political order made by a fundamentally unlimited sovereign power, built on the model of Cartesian theology. «Le prince est le Dieu cartésien transposé dans le monde politique.»[7] Doctrine of the ontological limitlessness of power. In perspective: 'reason of state' as defensive topos in favour of the logical autonomy of the political dimension in comparison with common human reason.

(*b*) 'Government' of the order of Being by God through logos in the form of general natural laws (*potentia Dei ordinata*). Problem of the relationship between general divine law (*lex aeterna*) and particular divine will (but can there be a 'particular' divine 'will'?).

(*b'*) Government of the social order through general political laws. Problem of the juridical relationship between positive general laws and provisions in individual cases.

(*c*) System of «uncreated essences» (Logos) co-eternal with God, conditioning the action of God as first efficient cause. (Epistemological essentialism, Leibniz's philosophy of idea-essences.)

(*c'*) System of fundamental principles of law and justice, posited as logical conditions of possibility of a juridical standardisation or of a political constitution. (Logical jusnaturalism, universalist transcendental ethics, political Platonism.)

(*d*) Ontology of potency: its modern theoretical climax in Spinoza's doctrine of God's infinite, necessary power as *natura naturans*, which produces the entire system of Being. Necessary concatenation of entities *sub specie æternitatis*; rigorously non-creationist and non-anthropomorphic framework. Infinite necessity.

(*d'*) Ontology of constituent power: doctrine of constituent power as potency, or original, permanent, inexhaustible political energy (Sieyès), which produces continually new institutional arrangements. Infinite will.

We must briefly examine these outlined analogies, bearing in mind that a truly adequate treatment of these topics would presuppose an as yet non-existent systematic treatment of the 'things' that lie behind the ambiguous lexical expression 'political theology'.

2. *Cartesian theology: creation and constitution.* – The Judeo-Christian thesis of creation as the work of a single all-powerful God is developed particularly by the nominalist theology of *potentia Dei absoluta* and ultimately finds in Descartes' God-as-'pure free will' its most trenchant philosophical formulation. The discriminating question is yet again: does God encounter in creation ontological limits owing to the structure of the 'thing itself' to be created, *vérités éternelles et necessaires*, as Leibniz says, or is he free

vis-à-vis Being, free – it is understood – even to change logos at will? The line of theological voluntarism, which runs from Duns Scotus/Ockham to Descartes (and continues, as de Muralt notes, up to that form of extreme theological voluntarism which is the existentialism of that Cartesian who was Sartre),[8] contrasts with the Platonic-Leibnizian epistemology of essences as *ideas of God capable of conditioning God.* Let us take a closer look at the two lines.

The process of neutralisation of the objective ethical *a priori* has its proper canonical place in the oft-mentioned passage of Ockham in which he argues that:

> the words 'theft', 'adultery', 'hatred', etc., do not designate these actions in an absolute sense, but only make known that the agent is obliged by divine commandment to do the opposite [. . .] If those actions were imposed by God, the agent would not be required to do the opposite, and then it would no longer be called theft, adultery, etc.[9]

It is clear that here the concepts of theft, adultery, etc. «*no longer designate any ethical-material quality of the action itself, but only the fact that that action is prohibited*»,[10] and consequently that if the prohibition is lifted they are no longer theft or adultery. «Bonitas moralis et malitia connotant, quod agens obligatur ad illum actum vel oppositum» (Ockham, *Sent.*, II, qu. 19 P). If the attribute of omnipotence, proper to God the creator, must be taken seriously, undoubtedly there is *in the actions themselves* no real good or evil, which corresponds to natural law, and that instead the ethical qualification of an action depends only on God's *praeceptum* (Ockham) or the sovereign's (Hobbes): ethical positivism underpins a theological positivism, and opens the way to a juridical positivism.

This process finds in Descartes its logical fulfilment: Descartes comes to subordinate – as Welzel observes[11] – even the principle of non-contradiction to God's omnipotence: God «did not want the sum of the angles of a triangle to be equal to two right angles because he recognised that it could not be otherwise, but on the contrary [. . .] because he wanted the three angles of the triangle to be necessarily equal to two right angles, this is true and cannot be otherwise.»[12] We face here the umpteenth argument of the *Euthyphro*: the laws subordinated to the ultimately arbitrary will of God *are not only the laws of ethics* – the hardly formalisable categories of good and evil – *but the very natural laws, logic and mathematics, could have been different if God had willed otherwise*. This is a marked radicalisation of the positions of Duns Scotus and Ockham, for whom the limit of the principle of non-contradiction remained valid without exception: the «logical impossibility» of propositions formally in contradiction. Welzel notes: «We face the seemingly paradoxical fact that the father of modern rationalism, Descartes, with respect to the problem of the ultimate foundation of the supreme practical and theoretical axioms, defends the maximum possible voluntarism. *Potentia Dei absoluta* becomes for him the absolute indifference of divine will. There is no good or truth whose idea had been in the divine intellect before the will of God decided to make it so.»[13]

From objective rule to subjective will. Therefore, «in itself 2 + 2 might make 5, anything might germinate spontaneously from nothing, two contradictions might both be true, the just might end up badly, it might be good to steal and kill».[14] Not so. The will is not arbitrary: it incorporates, as *potentia ordinata*, a residual form of logos that is a criterion of legality in an order *chosen by the potent subject*, man or God, who by acceding to free will belies the nature of artificer of an order. The fact is that, for Ockham as for Descartes, «there is in absolute no essentially good law, but only an essentially good legislator».[15]

This last remark is particularly important for an understanding of the complex dialectical relationship that always opposes logos, as universal blueprint of legality and rationality, and the will of the individual potent subject, author of the decision. While in Cartesian theology these two elements still overlap, assimilated in the figure of God as pure free will, the subsequent developments of political Cartesianism tend anew towards dissociation. A typical modern political philosopher such as Rousseau starts out from this Cartesian theology to then distort it into the construction of the extraordinary figure of the legislator that appears in the *Social Contract*.

The *'législateur'* is the personification of logos that provides the sovereign with outside inspiration, the latter being a perfect counterpart of God as mere executor who is the Platonic demiurge. In Rousseau the parallel lies between divine creation and the demiurgic constitution of a new political order – creation and constitution – both bearers of autonomous criteria of legitimacy and theodicy. In the famous chapter incipit of what is the most misinterpreted work (and source of misinterpretations) of the eighteenth century, Rousseau is the theologian of the dissociation between divine essence (legislator) and demiurgic action (sovereign):

> To discover the best rules of society suited to each Nation would require a superior intelligence who saw all of man's passions and experienced none of them, who had no relation to our nature yet knew it thoroughly, whose happiness was independent of us and who was nevertheless willing to care for ours [. . .]. It would require Gods to give men laws.
> [. . .] But if it is true that a great Prince is a rare man, what of a great Lawgiver? *The first need only follow the model which the other must propose. He is the scientist who invents the machine, the first is nothing but the workman who assembles it and operates it.*[16]

Rousseau's reproposal of Platonism thus takes the form of a dual analogy, which relates the two metaphorical areas of 'creation' and 'constitution' as follows:

It is up to the divine legislator, not the political sovereign, to «invent» the order – from among many possible

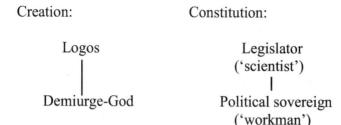

Creation: Constitution:

Logos   Legislator
                                    ('scientist')

Demiurge-God   Political sovereign
                                    ('workman')

orders – that is «worthy of being activated», neither more
nor less than is the impersonal structure of logos, not the
Demiurge-God, to provide the framework of intelligibility
of Being. The legislator then does not 'create' directly, but
rather provides the logical conditions of possibility for the
creation of the political order, and with it of Rousseau's
new man, having – as Rousseau puts it – the right to «alter
the constitution of man in order to reinforce it» (*Social
Contract*, II, 7). The sovereign political will that is inspired
by this logos is a general will that «loses its natural rec-
titude when it tends to some specific, individual object»,
because then – continues Rousseau – «judging about what
is alien to it, it lacks a true principle of equity capable
of guiding» (II, 4). Thus, from the principle by which
«there can be no general will on a specific object» (II,
6) there follows, because of Rousseau's apparent anti-
theological rationalism, the paradoxical need for a form
of theological-political occasionalism: «there must exist
occasional causes which set in motion the *lois générales*,
otherwise God would have to do it, and this would entail
in him a *volonté particulière*».[17]

The intellectual frameworks of political theology repro-
duce themselves by constantly new analogical transposi-
tions: there is a widespread return of the relationship
between general law as *ratio*, peculiar logos of a political
order, and individual modes of its realisation. Thus, it is
true in the theological context that God, in granting full
autonomy to the natural laws of Being as a closed and
self-sufficient system of *causae secundae*, still maintains

within his potency the faculty to intervene directly as *causa prima*, just as it is true in the political context that the sovereign can always decide, decreeing a «state of exception» to implement laws by suspending the form of the general law in order to ensure a *concrete* realisation of its substance. The dictator commissar would be in this case the embodiment in the juridical-political context of what «occasional cause» is in the theological context: typical figure of 'regional' logos which determines theologically the category of the Political.

3. *Leibniz and essences independent of God.* – Leibniz too still validates the principle of a scholastic-Cartesian «Deus potest immediate quidquid potest per causas secundas» metaphysics. As he states in his *Theodicy* (§ 392), «causae secundae agunt in virtute primae». But the meaning is quite different, because what Leibniz vigorously reaffirms beyond any occasionalist homage to theological voluntarism is the 'idealistic' line of the ethical, objective *a priori*.

God, then, can always intervene directly, skipping the circuit of second causes, but his action is conditioned by the essences that subsist *ab aeterno* in his intellect. These essences form the warp of 'possible' co-eternals with God (including – it must be stressed – even evil!), which God did not produce or want, but only 'found' in his own intellect. It is significant that § 183 of the *Theodicy*, which Leibniz devoted specifically to the very sensitive issue of the *nature of essences*, consists exclusively of a long quotation from Bayle – a philosopher anything but well disposed towards metaphysical idealism, but with whom Leibniz declares to agree without exception on this circumscribed subject matter, because of the exemplary clarity of its exposition. From this text the existence of God is entirely centred in the dialectic between the immutable essences (logos, whose creator is *not* God) and the decrees of his will, which does not determine the categories of ethics, but reflects them.[18] Here Leibniz-Bayle:

It is a certainty that the existence of God is not an effect of his will. He does not exist because he wants to exist, but for the needs of his infinite nature. His potency and science exist for the same need [. . .] The domain of his will does not regard the exercise of his potency, *and currently produces nothing outside of himself except what he wants, leaving everything else in a state of pure possibility.* It follows that his domain extends solely to the *existence* of creatures, while *not extending to their essences.* God was able to create matter, a man, a circle, or leave them as nothing, *but he could not produce them without their essential properties.* It was necessary for him to make man as a rational animal, and to give the circle a round shape, because, according to his ideas, eternal and independent of the free decrees of his will, the essence of man was made from the attributes of animality and rationality, and the essence of a circle from a circumference whose points are all equidistant from the centre. For this reason Christian philosophers recognised that the essences of things are eternal [. . .] and that therefore the essence of things and the truth of first principles are immutable. This is not to be understood as referring only to the first *theoretical* principles but also to first *practical* principles, and to all the propositions that contain the essence of all things.[19]

The passage concludes:

God saw from eternity, and with absolute necessity, the essential relationships of numbers, and the identity of the attribute and the subject in the propositions that contain the essence of everything. Likewise, *he saw that the word 'just' is implied in these other propositions: esteeming what is worthy of esteem, nurturing gratitude toward one's benefactor, fulfilling the terms of a contract, and so on, in several other propositions of morality.* It is therefore just to say [. . .] that man would be duty-bound to put into practice the content of those precepts even if God in his goodness had not ordained anything in reference to them. I would like you to pay attention to what, *if we go back with our abstractions to that ideal moment in which God had not yet decreed anything, we find in the ideas of God about the principles of morality, in terms that imply a duty.* [. . .] Now it seems clear why St Thomas Aquinas and Grotius were able to say that, even if there were no God, we would not be less obliged to conform to natural law. Others have said that, even if all the intelligences should perish, true propositions would remain such. Cajetan argued that, if he were left alone in the universe and if all things without exception were annihilated, the knowledge he had of the nature of a rose would not have ceased to exist.[20]

'Right' behaviour can therefore be recognised as corresponding to an immutable essence, *in mente Dei*, which comprises the *nature of the thing itself.* But evil too is an essence placed prior to the will of God: a 'possible' not created by God:

> Evil originates [. . .] from *forms* themselves when they are taken in the abstract; it originates, that is, from the ideas that God *has not produced by an act of his will*, as he did with numbers and figures, as well, in a word, as with all possible essences, which we must consider eternal and necessary. All these essences *are located in the ideal region of the possible, that is, in the divine intellect.* God, therefore, *is not at all the author of essences which in any degree are nothing but possibilities.*[21]

One wonders: but is it once again God's will, not his intellect, that is the discriminating element for qualifying the ethics of human behaviour? Prior to God's 'existentifying' will, the essence of 'good' and the essence of 'evil', the essence of 'right' and the essence of 'wrong' are nothing more than possibilities placed formally on the same level in the divine intellect. It is God's will that, even if it does not prevent evil from coming into existence, opts judiciously for the essence of 'good' or 'right' by deciding to bring it into being. If, however – with Leibniz – we exclude Descartes' theological voluntarism, on what basis can that essence be declared 'good' or 'right'? Or: *why*, ultimately, is the essence of 'good' or 'right' called 'good' or 'right'? There is no definitive answer to this question. Examples of acts in conformity with just reason or the «nature of the thing' («esteeming what ought to be esteemed, doing good for good, doing no evil to anyone, giving everyone his due»)[22] reveal a facile lapse into tautology: such-and-such behaviour is right because it corresponds to the nature of the thing, and the nature of the thing is right. It is right because it is right. But evil too – it was said – since it is an essence in the mind of God, falls (and cannot but fall) within the concept of the nature of the «mind-thing» of God.[23]

In fact, the essences found *in mente Dei* prior to the existence of their corresponding things are axiologically of every kind, as is recognised in § 335 itself of the *Theodicy*. The judgement by which God *judiciously chooses* the 'good' essences, judging them worthy of existence and thus bringing them *directly* into existence through an act of will, is the same judgement by which God draws indirectly into existence the essences of evil connected to the divine plan of activation of the same possible order.

What remains then of the concrete ontological connotation of action as 'right' action? What are the concrete connotations of this justice of his? *Congruitas ac proportionalitas*, responds Leibniz: congruence and proportionality.[24] These features, however, are purely formal, in a word: empty. So Welzel's exact observation:

When Leibniz, in his *Monita* to Pufendorf, refers, as evidence of the *a priori* content of justice that this maintains certain laws of equality and proportionality ('*aequalitatis proportionalitatisque leges*') [. . .] he mentions without doubt the only valid *a priori* principle that the doctrine of natural law had been able to determine as the content of justice since Aristotle, a principle of a purely formal nature! What Kant says of logic, that it had made no progress since Aristotle, is even more valid for natural law; since Aristotle introduced the concept of equality into the concept of justice, no further *a priori* valid content has been added to the concept of law.[25]

There are insurmountable difficulties in Leibniz's system. Difficulties that nevertheless do not diminish the great impact of the idealist current in the history of natural law theory: from Plato to the Stoics, via Christianity and Aquinas's reading of Aristotle, down to Leibniz and beyond, a whole school of thought agrees in affirming that «there are just things prior to God's decrees» (*Theodicy*, § 182). And here it must be acknowledged that Leibniz, contrary to what Welzel asserts, exerted a profound influence on what would be the metaphysical presuppositions of the secular Enlightenment: the general principles of law that would find their place in the European codes, as well as in the American constitutional movement – both movements based on the idea that the rationality of the law can be ontologically founded.[26] «*Avant qu'il y eût des lois faites, il y avait des rapports de justice possibles*», Montesquieu declared conclusively, expressing himself by no coincidence in that axiomatic form which often stamps the circuit of reason with authoritative finality.[27] The fact remains that this phrase of Montesquieu's is an incisive summation of the arc of idealist metaphysical thought: that thought which – from Aquinas to Leibniz, by focusing attention on the *complexio oppositorum* of 'possible' essences – had constituted the greatest obscuration of the philosophical topic of substance-potency.

4. *Spinoza and the inadmissibility of a «theological constitutionalism».* – Spinoza's metaphysics take quite a different turn. The central problem for Spinoza is to construct Being as a field of forces, made up of modifications of the

power expressed by a single immanent substance. There is lacking from the outset all trace of Leibniz's plurality of possible, separate, heroic essences along with God, inasmuch as constitutive principles of his logos. The idea of such a personal God as 'existentificator' of logoi-essences would reek, for Spinoza, of naive anthropomorphism sustained by a Platonic-Christian prejudice. For Spinoza there is no room for dualistic constructs, traceable to the final opposition between Logos and Being: on the contrary, if we wish to speak of logos, we must see in it the simple logical form, axiologically empty, that describes the movements and tensions of finite modes of Being within the infinite substance-potency of *natura naturans*. Logos does not reflect, platonically, a good or a transcendence, and not even some sort of *will*;[28] it is pure formula of comprehension, algorithm, of what inevitably, necessarily takes place and develops according to immanent rules.

In this sense, we can perhaps say that the Spinozan 'model' is a *tertium genus* with regard to the essentialism/ conventionalism dilemma. Spinozan substance has nothing of the Platonic *essence*, which migrates to the personal Christian God and onward to Leibniz;[29] but it does not even simply dissolve into the *convention* posed by some potent will (theological positivism), or find a place in the impersonal fabric of languages (and therefore expression of the context of semantics + culture + history proper to modern anthropological relativism). Substance is the *natura naturans* already given since always, producing all individual forms, which are simple modifications of it.

There is consequently no space for the blueprint of a political theology, if by this term we mean, as we have done, the «analogy of potency» between a personal God and the source of political power. Political theology, Spinoza would say, feeds on *imagination* and *mythology*: it is defined as the area in which the human imagination applies itself to the problem of the legitimacy of worldly systems, projecting into it teleological and anthropomorphic deformations:

We see that all the notions with which common people are wont to explain nature are only ways of imagining, and do not indicate the nature of anything, but only the constitution of the imagination; and since they have names, almost of entities existing outside of the imagination, I call them entities of imagination and not entities of reason.[30]

The entire *Tractatus Theologico-Politicus* is, on close inspection, a refutation of political theology as the area of analogy between the two potencies, human and divine; and various points of his *Ethics* confirm this view:

Common people understand God's potency as his free will, and his right over all things that are, which therefore are considered contingent. They say that God has the power to destroy everything and reduce it to nothing. Further, *they compare very often the potency of God with that of a king*. But we have refuted this [. . .]: we have shown that God acts with the same necessity he applies to himself; that is: just as from the same necessity of his divine nature it follows (as all unanimously confirm) that God applies to himself, by the same necessity it also follows that God makes infinite things in infinite ways [. . .].

Wishing to continue with this topic, I could also prove that the kind of potency that common people attribute falsely to God is not only human (which shows that God is conceived by common people as a man or in the guise of a man), but actually implies impotence [. . .] *And no one can really grasp what I mean unless he is careful not to confuse God's potency with human potency or with the right of kings.*[31]

Political theology is nonetheless a *real* knowledge, since the human imagination is real and productive of 'real' effects, taking it as its proper subject or symbolic material of play. In this sense Spinoza does not proceed to a total, indiscriminate demystification: he does not go so far as to deny the usefulness of an analysis of the argumentational processes inspired by theological-political analogy in the various areas of practical human knowledge. This perspective remains simply outside his purview of interest, which instead is focused on the task of achieving the rational demonstration of his ontology. In other words, the Spinozan destruction of the 'truth' of theological-political analogy does not in the least affect the 'validity' of political theology as a sociology of juridical concepts (especially regarding the concept of 'sovereignty').[32]

There is no doubt that this latter field of research reveals the confusion (but at the same time the actual productivity of confusion) between the concepts of *power* and *potency*. Human beings, to act, turn more often than not unconsciously to a dense array of concepts and symbologies of theological origin, which reflect the fundamental analogy between political power and the potency of God. The very idea of *reason of state*, which developed in the heart of modern thought as a vindication of the autonomous character of the logic of political power, in keeping with common human reason, took shape as the complete, definitive secularised version of the idea of *God's omnipotence*. Underlying both is the intuition of the natural limitlessness of power, so that it appears illusory to focus theoretical attention – as, for example, in the modern era, liberal constitutionalism has done – on the juridical techniques of the containment of power itself, seeing in them the ontological foundation of a 'naturally' limited State.[33]

It is possible, in my opinion, to interpret Spinoza by insisting on the continuity that links potency as a principle of the constitution of the *individual subject* (or the potency of the mind, the human quest for the maximum possible increase of reality as conservation and completion of its nature) and potency as a principle of the constitution of the *collective subject* («*multitudo*»: potency of the multitude that «is guided as by a single mind»).[34] The error of Platonism is for Spinoza precisely that of conceiving of the real essence as something static, a forever unchanging nature of the thing given, in which every entity participates through similarity or imitation, on the basis of a sort of unconditional having to be. On the contrary, the reality of an entity must be seen as determined dynamically by the «degree of completion» which that entity embodies, and it unfolds therefore as a continuous process of *attribution of being* (or, negatively, as a defect of being). The human world of meaning is representable as a circuit of increment (or decrement) of completion of individual entities within a horizon of complete immanence (this topic, on the dynamics of «*affectus*», is precisely the subject of Parts III, IV and V of the *Ethics*). There is, in a word, no «nature of things», but a free development of the potency of entities.

Thus in the 'political' sphere the quest for a constitutional formula that guarantees a definitive limitation of power-potency is inadmissible. It is absolutely false that this limitation can be inherent to the nature of the power-thing and that therefore potency lends itself 'naturally' to be channelled into institutional forms of containment. Constitutionalism is thus reclassified to its non-ontological character of simple technique and ideology, unlike what the philosophy that had determined its origins believed it to be.[35]

5. *Schmitt's interpretation of Spinoza: the link between* «*constitutive potency*» *and* «*constituent power*». – This, as a disenchanted analysis of the phenomenon of potency in its peculiar legality and in its tendency to a natural expansion, is perhaps the greatest indication contained in Spinoza's philosophy: an indication immediately translatable into theoretical-political terms as a criticism of every ideology that contemplates the 'naturally limited' character of power.

It is on this particular note that Carl Schmitt's interpretation of Spinoza becomes highly significant.[36] Spinoza and Schmitt: two distant and seemingly incommunicable universes (the Jewish liberal and the Catholic reactionary, in the two-dimensional triteness of the history of political thought) reconnect in a common criticism of the political theology of secularisation, or – better yet – in the common appreciation of constituent power as primary political reality, from which the non-theological positivity of power descends (i.e. the non-objectifiable, non-regulatable logos of potency).[37]

It is a line of *political anti-Platonism* opposed to the substantialist metaphysics of law (which we find in the implicit Kantianism of contemporary liberals), and opposed to what we previously called «theological constitutionalism», a mirror of the having to be of a power that is ostensibly self-limited, superimposed on the ontological materiality of potency.

If there is no longer room, in the theoretical reconstruction of the logos of politics, for immutable natural-law essences or «eternal truths», what deserves attention in a realistic way – by using Schmitt's methodology of sociological analysis of juridical concepts and, inseparably, Spinoza's remarks about the ontology of potency – is the essence of constituent power as an ontological device that gives origin to potency in history. As «non-organisable organiser principle»[38] this figure of constituent power lays a fresh claim, distorting them, to the characteristic properties of the idea of God's omnipotence.

Let us then consider two of Schmitt's texts in which he devotes significant attention to this issue on the genealogical reconstruction of the concept of constituent power. We notice at once that the names that appear in these texts are those of Spinoza (the radical, necessitarist Spinoza) and Sieyès (the radical voluntarist Sieyès), who represent the two versions – approval and opposition – of what we might call the «positive theory» of constituent power.

> The relationship between *pouvoir constituant* and *pouvoir constitué* has its most perfect systematic, methodological analogy in the relationship between *natura naturans* and *natura naturata*, an idea that has found a place even in the rationalistic system of Spinoza but that, for this very

reason, shows that that system is not purely rational. The same must be said of the doctrine of *pouvoir constituant*, which in vain tries to be understood in terms of pure mechanistic rationalism. The people, the nation, the original force of any state entity, generate constantly new organs. From the infinite and unfathomable abyss of its power arise ever new forms, which it can break when it wants and in which it never definitively crystallises its power.[39]

In certain of Sieyès' statements *pouvoir constituant*, in its relationship with all *pouvoirs constitués*, appears in a metaphysical analogy with *natura naturans* and its relationship with *natura naturata* in terms of Spinoza's doctrine: an inexhaustible first cause of all forms, itself not containable in any form, which draws out of itself eternally new forms, which creates all forms informally [. . .]. However, it is necessary to distinguish from that pantheistic metaphysics his positive theory of constituent power, which is part of every doctrine of constitution; the two things are not at all identical to each other. The metaphysics of *potestas constituens* as an analogous instance of *natura naturans* is part of the theory of political theology.[40]

As is readily apparent, both texts contain some differences, especially about the way in which the reference to the theological-political analogy is presented and evaluated. While the first text merely states the validity of the «systematic and methodological analogy» between Sieyès' *pouvoir constituant* – *pouvoir constitué* pair and Spinoza's *natura naturans* – *natura naturata* pair, the second text establishes the need for a distinction between what is called Spinoza's «pantheistic metaphysics» and his «positive theory of constituent power», which Schmitt recognises in its purer form in Sieyès.[41]

To say, as Schmitt does at the end of the second text, that «the two things are not at all identical» means emphasising once again the extraneousness of Spinoza's ontological

monism in relation to the necessarily dualistic constructions of political theology – constructions inspired by the
full transcendence of the source of political power no less
than of the deity. Spinoza's philosophy – Schmitt means –
is a far cry from both Descartes' and Malebranche's philos-
ophies, both inspired by Christian metaphysical dualism
and by the sharp contrast between creature and creator.
The infinite and omnipotent «personal-subject-God» of
Christian theology deprives his creatures of any *original-
ity of potency*: in political theology, that means deducing
metaphysically the inevitability of delegating power – in
a word, representation. Thus the Prince is the sole representative of the totality of power in the political world, just
as God is the only guarantor of the truth and objectivity
of logical relationships in the natural world. The constitutive dualism that characterises the Christian theology of
Descartes and Malebranche obviously concerns also the
radically reformed Christianity of Hobbes, which Schmitt
assumes as a prototype of the theological-political structure of thought of the modern State.

Spinoza's philosophy cannot be identified with the
dualistic patterns of political theology, to begin with
for the simple reason that he substitutes the dialectic of
Hobbesian «truth/authority» with the hermeneutics of
sole substance or immanent power, absolutely invariable
in terms of analogy. A hypothetical «Spinozan crystal» –
never explicitly developed by Schmitt[42] – in place of the
analogy (between a transcendent God and a sovereign individual power) sees the *identity* (of God and Being, *natura
naturans* and *natura naturata*).

In conclusion, we can say that it is the constituent power
of the symbolic entity that contains the *logos of politics*,
understood as logos of the natural potency of the *multitudo* of humanity. No Platonic-Christian transcendence of
'objective logos-rule' with respect to the formless aggre-
gate of natural Being is in this sense admissible. It would
be in vain, then, in the Spinozan perspective of the logos of
potency (where the genitive, we said, is only subjective) to

fret over a claimed «theological constitutionalism»: about a construct, that is, which implies a fundamental dualism between subject and rules – between 'potent subject' and 'objective rules'.

With this last point in mind, let us return to the question that prompted us from the start (Chapter I, § 6). We return to it with a justifiably negative answer: if «natural potency» must exist and be valid as a hermeneutic criterion of human actions, this potency provides by itself its own rules and its own 'logos', which therefore it does not find outside of itself, as separate essences.

Constituent power *versus* theological constitutionalism: there is no objective ethical logos that limits *a priori* the potency of the living. The living has already in itself its own ethics of natural potency, which is channelled into the forms which are proper to it, inspired by a logic of growth. It is an ethics of natural passions (of *affectus*) that cannot simply be repressed, that must instead be appreciated, directed, and – above all – *interpreted*. The task of this interpretation involves a logos-function which, in contrast to every logos-substance, is largely pure algorithm of the movements (and «passions») of the living. And this by *recognising* certainly in nature the effectivity and operativity of analytical truths (those truths that appear such «in all possible worlds», or «in all worlds which have verified conditions of rationality», dependent in turn on the existence of an evolved human mind), but *excluding* the claim to deduce in the sphere of practical action any universal rules of having to be.[43]

However, the analytical structure of the logos of potency (which in its deepest essence is being, not having to be) constantly eludes us. The description of its minute articulations, the knowledge of its autonomous legality, clearly constitutes a chapter that, as outlined by Spinoza and later reprised intermittently by Nietzsche in his *Posthumous Fragments*, has yet to be written.

V

Genealogies of Constituent Potency: Schmitt, Nietzsche, Spinoza

1. *Analogies and genealogies.* – There is a profound analogy between the historical and intellectual position of Nietzsche, located, according to Heidegger's well-known diagnosis, at the end of the history of Western metaphysics, and the position of Schmitt, whose work marks the end of the modern history of European jurisprudence: of the great centuries-old tradition of *jus publicum Europaeum*. The analogy is not superficial: it invests in both cases the epistemological field, to the point of touching on the very ways of conceiving the idea of rationality.

What acquires in this connection an absolutely transparent meaning is the supremacy, as affirmed in hermeneutics, of the 'who' (i.e. the interpreting subject in Nietzsche, the deciding subject in Schmitt) over the 'what' (i.e. the interpreted fact in Nietzsche, the normative content of the decision in Schmitt). It appears that Nietzsche's fundamental thesis, according to which the aim of knowledge is not reducible positivistically to a simple 'fact' (just as the subject of knowledge is not Kantianly traceable to a transcendental entity), has a direct counterpart in Schmitt's decisionistic epistemology, it too overstepping the methodological canons of philosophical (and scientific) rationalism.

Other clear 'structural' analogies between the two authors are discoverable in relation to the *genealogical method* inaugurated by Nietzsche, which definitively abandoned all naive forms of juxtaposition with constructions of morality and pursued a factual-historical research into the criteria of formation (considered by Nietzsche as most often 'contemptible') of moral judgements, not unlike the way Schmitt, in getting past the positivistic prohibition, restores full dignity to the genealogical analysis of the prejuridical «origins» of law in the «concept» of law itself. To Nietzsche's genealogical analysis of morals, reflected in the great tradition of Western metaphysics, thus corresponds Schmitt's genealogical analysis of the political essence, in the strong sense, of the law, reflected in the equally great tradition of European jurisprudence.[1]

2. *Natural potency and constituent power.* – If the impossibility of enclosing natural potency in the illusory rationality of form is one of Nietzsche's central themes, which prompted Deleuze's famous signalling of the influence of Spinoza,[2] it is in my opinion the concept of *constituent power* that marks the place where the Nietzschean-Spinozan ontology of potency enters fruitfully into relation – very interestingly – with Schmitt's juridical-political theorising. The notion of constituent power has the function, we might say, of an ontological device, namely the mechanism of foundation of new material horizons of meaning (irreducible to the legal-political field in which, nevertheless, they directly disclose themselves), and this in complete independence with respect to the form taken by the powers constituted within the given normative framework.

The first corollary to be derived from the notion of constituent power is its «imperishability»: the circumstance that – as Schmitt puts it – it «is not finite and eliminated by the fact of having once been exercised»,[3] but that «next to and above its constitution the constituent will continues to exist»,[4] which – be it said in passing – renders quite unreliable theses about the supposed «exhaustion» of constituent power in modern constitutional democracies, although these continue to have a certain appeal in the debate within Italian constitutional doctrine.[5]

The fact is that we witness regularly, in juridical science, but also in practical politics when efforts at normalisation prevail in it, what we might call the 'tabooisation' of origins, a clear sign of which is the singular reticence and 'selective blindness' on the part of interpreters most closely tied to the status quo in the description of the genetic moment of constitution. This precisely where it would be fitting to *call by name* the real forces intervening in the founder game. (However, we might think that the so-called «taboo about the origins of an order» does not depend so much, or only, on the merely opportunistic behaviour of the interpreters, but rather implies – far more seriously – what on an epistemological level is recognised as the impossibility of describing fully within a given paradigm the rules that presided over its formation: describing them would require being already outside of that paradigm!)

It is what the most alert jurists indirectly admit when they say that constitutions in reality hold up «on a tacit but well-defined agreement»: about which none of the acting forces in them want to raise the question of sovereignty.[6] The genealogical question of sovereignty – of the unnameable origin of the order in the language internal to that very order – thus becomes the warning light of the constitutive weakness of any power structure. Every procedure of institutionalisation is, so to speak, undermined in its foundations by the unspeakableness of the powers that founded it. The question, as those same jurists candidly acknowledge, is thus «evaded, but certainly not resolved».[7]

3. *Counterforces.* – Pitting, as do the supporters of the «theory of exhaustion» of constituent power, the *rights of man* against the constituent power, considering that the thinkability of the latter fails when the assertion of such rights is taken seriously, is once again political theology, as is also political theology the theory in itself of human rights, seen as a new 'immutable', whose 'eternity' is actually the result of a resacralisation. We stand, with the liberal-universalist doctrine of the rights of man, before one more revival of political-theological dogma, which refurbishes, transposing it into a new area of application – this time (and not just figuratively) of planetary extension

– the Enlightenment utopia of the *civitas maxima*.[8] But critical thinking cannot be exempted from concluding, even in political theory, its job of unmasking and demystifying, comforted in this, in truth, by the rise of a new awareness in the most alert sectors of society, no longer willing to submit passively to the planetary ideological dominance of universalist political theology, which conceals behind the reasonings of philosophical monism the desire (unspeakable, but all-too-present) to flatten and standardise the constitutive cultural differences among life forms.

In this sense it must be said that a particularly damaging strategic role is played by the convergence, now perceivable at all levels, between monism in philosophy (rhetorics of the '*pensée unique*' globalist perspective), monotheism in religion (the primacy of the institutionalised Christianity of the Church of Rome) and socio-ethical, egalitarian universalism.

But there exist, as I said, counterforces. Thus, one cannot but agree with Gianfranco Miglio about the increasingly open challenge, with liberating effects, of «the old, acritically accepted belief that being standardised and sacrificing one's singularity and diversity on the altar of a mythical, egalitarian "unity" is a higher duty: a "value" binding on all others».[9] Just as another classic dogma of the same *jus publicum Europaeum* is being challenged, one that stands traditionally alongside standardisation: I refer to the dogma of the so-called 'timelessness' of the political order in its existing form, that is, the State-form. By virtue of this alleged dogma, Miglio goes on, the minority that asks to dissolve the bonds of loyalty (and thus of political obligation) by which it was incorporated perhaps centuries ago into a broader institutional aggregation, would commit an unforgivable crime, lacerating and killing a living creature (!) by reclaiming its «right of individual secession». This when it is by now sufficiently clear – and on this, public opinion itself very often winds up agreeing – that «political coexistence can no longer be based on terms of fidelity – a life-and-death oath, and therefore "eternal" – but secularly on fixed-term "contracts", "conditioned" and therefore destined, at some point, to being renegotiated, or to being dissolved and allowing the parties to be free».[10]

A realistic analysis thus overturns the dogmas – dear to the self-preserving logic of power – of the standardisation and timelessness of institutions, while the unitary notion – of metaphysical and theological origin – of political obligation is called seriously into question by the libertarian argument which affirms the transience of any constraint before the will, expressed by anyone, «to stand with whomever one wants»,[11] and therefore before the right (pre-political, and therefore imprescriptible) to review periodically the reasons on which political coexistence is founded.

4. *Hypothesis.* – Our hypothesis – as mentioned before – is that only by going backwards on the line of the genealogical method, from Schmitt through Nietzsche to Spinoza, is it possible to trace the initial theoretical framework from which, at the start of modernity, the logic of constituent power had its origin as an ontological dissolver device of every transcendence of power.

If *self-referentiality* is the primary danger typical of contemporary political systems, such as to produce in them a potential for self-legitimation that increasingly disregards any control by individuals, to the point of accomplishing a complete neutralisation of consent,[12] the answer to this involutive mechanism cannot but entail a profound theoretical re-estimation of the role played by the *natural potency* of individuals.

It is, in other words, Spinoza's *potency* of individual wills that, democratically organised «as one mind» (Spinoza, *Tractatus Politicus*, III, 2), is directed against power seen as a general institutional reality, engulfing but inflexible, because never willing to rationally call into question the logical premises of its operation. Never as now, when the *liberal*, or ex-socialist, universalist ideologies have generally taken the seats of power in the West,[13] do the appropriation of the State and the strengthening of the powers-that-be signify the expropriation of the potency of individuals and the rejection of any instance of constituent power. Hence, new lines of resistance and new friend/foe demarcations, along strategic paths whose development cannot as yet be foreseen but whose scope is already quite clear, definable perhaps in Foucaultian terms as 'biopolitics': what is at issue is the organisation of life itself, which becomes the *direct* object of political action.

The strategy of power, whose «strategic concept» makes it artificer of a definite global power, achieves at this point an ever more pervasive impact: the natural potencies of individuals are *forces* that must be continually neutralised and sublimated into the universalist and transcendental dimensions of the communities of communication. As Deleuze masterfully explains, the goal of this strategy is to «separate the active force (individual potency) from its object: from that on which it exercises its power», and thus «to dispossess it» as a force. In line with this analysis, it is again of course Nietzsche – the Nietzschean genealogy – that intervenes to «analyze in detail how such a separation is possible [. . .]: always through separation and division, since the reactive forces do not triumph by forming a superior force, but by means of a pretence they separate active force from that over which it exercises its power».[14]

5. *Against any normativist universalism.* – The theoretical-political concept of constituent power thus refers necessarily to an «analytics of forces», meaning by this expression the sociological forces that resist their demotion, at the hands of juridical science, to the rank of established power. In this sense the value and utility of Carl Schmitt's contribution in reference to the «constitutionalist zeroing» of the concept of constituent power is quite clear.[15] True, Schmitt still proceeds within the ponderous ideology of *jus publicum Europaeum*, but – it might be added – declares its fulfilment after having thoroughly tested the possibility.

Here we see clearly the full extent of the «will to truth»

of a viewpoint that, while taking charge of the design of dominance typical of the classical doctrine of sovereignty, nevertheless has no intention of reducing its role to that of instrument of control and segmentation (tending towards zero) of constituent power. Carl Schmitt seems to say that within juridical science – but a juridical science oriented very differently from the dominant normativist universalism – there may still be room for the comprehension of phenomena such as original constituent power. Here he refers to other authors who «as jurists» confirm the cognitive value of juridical science (and especially the science of public law) when this is not reduced to an empty technology of power.[16]

But, as has been accurately observed about the risks of a possible institutionalist involution, «*that potency, being institutionalised, cannot fail to negate itself*, seems an initial, irreducible affirmation of importance [. . .]: well beyond the defensive commonplaces of contemporary institutionalism, any philosophy that even heroically reaches institutionalist conclusions must be rejected if we want to embrace the potency of the constituent principle».[17] Institutionalism, in other words, is a kind of idealistic elaboration of the theme of constituent power: an elaboration that, compared to obtuse positivist negation, undoubtedly has the merit of not dismissing from the start the question of origins, though only to transfer it into a sort of pacified situation of whose non-conflictual outcome its dialectic is guarantor.

I think, in conclusion, that the analytical value of Schmitt's concept of constituent power can be maintained,[18] notwithstanding our awareness of its inseparability from the context of its formation (which remains the classical doctrine of *jus publicum Europaeum*). Which, rather than implying a diminution of the cognitive scope of his concept, further enhances its meaning; for not everything that originates within a concept exhausts its sphere of validity in that context; rather, its criterion of validity is often recognisable precisely because of its capacity for extra-contextual application.

The theological-political origin of the modern concept of constituent power, from Sieyès to Schmitt, therefore in no way compromises its productivity as an irreplaceable instrument of scientific analysis. Nevertheless, it must – and this is the task of a possible future *political anthropology* (which will have to be resolutely anti-universalistic) – connect its subject matter to that of the Spinozan-Nietzschean concept of natural potency, and adopt the latter, on a theoretical-political terrain, as a propulsive element of the idea of constituent will, that the theory of the 'political' – hastily declared by contemporary technocratic universalism, deteriorated or perhaps even obsolete – necessarily revokes.

Threshold

The human mind has phased out its traditional anchorage in a natural biological basis (the «reasons of the body» which even Spinoza's *Ethics* could count on) – an anchorage that had determined, for at least two millennia, historically familiar forms of culture and civilisation. Increasingly emphasising its intellectual disembodiment, it has come to the point of establishing in a completely artificial way the normative conditions of social behaviour and the very ontological collocation of human beings in general. If in the past 'God' was the name that mythopoietic activity had assigned to the world's overall moral order, which was reflected onto human behaviour, now the progressive freeing of the mind – by way of the intellectualisation of life and technology – from the natural normativity which was previously its basic material reference opens up unforeseen vistas of power. Freedom of the intellect demands (or so one believes) the full artificiality of the normative human order in the form of an artificial logos, and precisely qua artificial, omnipotent. The technological icon of logos (which postmodern dispersion undermines only superficially) definitively unseats the traditional normative, sovereign 'God' of human history as he has been known till now. Our West has been irreversibly marked by this process, whose results are as devastating as they are inevitable. The decline predicted a century ago by old Spengler is here served on a platter.

The first corollary which follows briefly reconstructs the modern origins of this ineluctable path – simultaneously historical and epistemological – towards the conventionality/artificiality of the idea of order. The second corollary seeks to indicate, by digging genealogically backwards, the theological-political concept of order that, willy-nilly, has characterised our Western civilisation over the past millennium. The third corollary examines in an openly critical way one of the most representative intellectual developments – that of Habermas – which has nourished in recent years the universalist philosophical narrative of the West.

Corollaries

Corollary I

On the Origins of Conventionalist Political Philosophy in the Seventeenth Century

At the basis of any consideration about the modern state of experience lie concepts of great theoretical and practical import, such as the dialectic between private and public, 'internal' and 'external', essence and appearance, which only a historiographic-philosophical investigation into the origins of the new conventionalistic concept of political order allows us to clarify. I will endeavour, therefore, in the following notes, to focus on the theoretical elements that the new political anthropology injected into the circuitry of sixteenth-century Europe, thanks especially to key thinkers such as Montaigne and Charron, convinced as I am of their thematic relevance in the context of a closer analysis of that phenomenon of primary importance now called, to use Benjamin's term, the 'crisis experience'.

1. *Introversion.* – The movement that, through Montaigne, was accomplished by the Western spirit, turning inward on itself in the 'inner provinces' of moral criticism, and retreating before the impossibility of exerting an effectual dominion over the world, is a reality not without political consequences, such as to bring about truly momentous discontinuities. I believe that three essential problematic nuclei, implicit in the concept just expressed, can be outlined.

They are: *a*) the presence of a metaphysical entity in the European spirit, whose analysis breaks down into psychologistic tones (its typical form being the Montaigne-style *essai*), but recognising itself as modern precisely in that, and situated subsequent to the loss of that ideal 'aura' which the humanist spirit had created and conserved; *b*) a movement towards introversion by individual subjectivity, which, reflecting upon itself, led necessarily to an attitude of sceptical relativism; *c*) a feature in a political sense of this movement towards introversion/reflection that, far from being a simple escape from the world, determined a quantum shift in the modes of perceiving ethical-political experience.[1] The inner development of the individual, the fulfilment of his *Bildung*, required, on a political level, protection from outside, resulting in the legitimation of new organisational patterns of state power by reason of the security they procure.

There was a profound connection between this 'turning inward', which originated with modern conventionalistic political philosophy, and the disenchanted experience of libertine nihilism. Libertine experience refused to exploit in absolute, metahistorical terms the forms of dominion that loomed on the horizon of modernity. The libertine learned from Montaigne that one must nevertheless adhere in some way *in interiore sphaera* to ensure one's individual 'inner' development. The spirit thus referred to what historically existed, and in so referring, accepted it: from Montaigne to Charron and Naudé, the relationship of the isolated individual to juridical-political institutions preserved and amplified the problematic character of this acceptance. In any case, it is an acceptance endured, suffered, and libertine thought never made pretense of a harmonious correspondence between the value of the individual and the value of the State. The libertine defence of order, which at first glance might appear to be a happy solution to this 'suffering', was skin-deep, more superficial with respect to theory; the fact remains that in spite of its ancillary, subordinate character, the defence of order found itself at times at odds with the negative thought that developed within the individual, with which it established a paradoxical coexistence. But the moral critique carried out by negative thinking had no immediate political effects. As long as it remained strictly circumscribed within the individual's inner sphere, sufficient leeway remained for a conventional obedience to external rules.

Reinhart Koselleck has had the merit of carrying out a precise, in-depth historical analysis of the relationship between the criticism developed by negative thought and the crisis of existing institutional systems, by showing how the disorderly emergence of conflict provoked, between the seventeenth and eighteenth centuries, on the one hand an eruption of moral criticism from meta-phorical 'inner' space, and on the other the intrusion of this same criticism in the political sphere, in the form of the Enlightenment philosophy of history.[2] Koselleck, in the dense first chapter of his work, significantly entitled «The political structure of Absolutism as a premise of the Enlightenment', finds Hobbes in the forefront of the problem. But Hobbes's thought presents significant analogies here, for example, precisely in the distinction between *interior* and *exterior sphaera* with the sceptical, libertine the-oretical framework of early seventeenth-century France, patterned on Montaigne's thought.[3]

It might be said that in this respect the libertine rep-resented the first stage of a process that would reveal, in its 'last acts', the disruptive effects of the Enlightenment philosophy of history: he represented, that is, the moment in which the subdivision between the metaphorical spaces of internal criticism and external delegation began to advance as a necessary condition for the establishment of a legal, juridical political system of a conventional nature.

The 'phenomenology of the libertine' revolved around the turning in on itself of the sceptical soul: this was the act which founded the inner space of criticism, the pre-requisite of the recognition of conventionality/relativity of every external value. The Montaigne-Charron-Naudé line clearly reproduced this awareness, which, as we have said, in no way lessened the need to adhere to the value of the modern State, as it would be theorised more maturely by Hobbes. (Between the sceptical-libertine group and the theoretical one of mature absolutism, Sorbière was perhaps – *geistesgeschichtlich* – the element of union.)

Pintard demonstrates as characteristic the fact that libertine scepticism, in its flamboyant defence of the whims of rulers, went beyond the fiercest needs of absolutism,[4] leading precisely those who relativistically no longer believed in its value to become, in historical contingency, the most ruthless supporters of the enhancing of the coercive structures of the State. The instrumentality of the libertine position seems to hark back to certain typical passages in Montaigne (see for example *Essais*, II, XVII). Of course, the distance from Montaigne became unbridgeable when the libertines proposed, beyond any immobilism, a distinctly radical political behaviour, revealing themselves in this «*audacieux et décidés*», «*à l'extrême pointe conquérante du mouvement absolutiste*».[5] But we should perhaps note that it was precisely here, at the point where Montaigne's moderation overturned into its opposite, into a clear-cut, determined action for the sake of an instrumental purpose, that the positive fruits of sceptical conventionalism were yielded, in eighteenth-century bourgeois practice. The origin of this form of thought is to be sought in Montaigne, and therefore it is with Montaigne that we shall begin our analysis of the crisis that the perception of the ethical-political experience encountered and underwent in the early seventeenth century.

2. *Disorder.*

> Travelling one day, my brother Seigneur de la Brousse and I, during our civil wars, met a well-mannered gentleman who belonged to the party opposed to ours, but we knew nothing of this, as he dissembled it. The worst of these wars is that the cards get shuffled to the point where your enemy seems so like you in everything: in language, deportment, customs, that it is difficult to avoid confusion and disorder.[6]

This passage from Montaigne is doubtless among the most telling in its indication of the complex historical context in which the sceptical criticism of experience situated itself, in that particularly representative moment of the phenomenology of modernity which the civil wars of religion constituted. In this passage every 'aura' has already disappeared completely: he «belonged to the party opposed to ours [. . .], he dissembled it». The civil wars of religion displayed the distinctively modern feature of total war: the fact that an undecipherable system of signs concealed the reality of a world populated by unknown and unknowable enemies. In this context human aggressiveness found uncontrolled release, and what remained of rational humanist decorum, of the security that is necessary for life, degenerated into a bundle of illusory experiences.[7]

«Now we no longer know if our neighbour is friend or foe, and if he who presents himself as friend or foe is in truth that» (*Essais*, II, V). The greatest danger comes from what is equal to us and hides behind the signs of this equality, once a guarantee of social coexistence, now mere insidiousness, *«piège»*. Signs no longer correspond to things, but rather, in a state of exception, turn real relationships on their heads. The historical-political situation of civil war is the paradigm of this far more widespread and alarming logical situation.

The extent to which signs lead to an insidious, hostile terrain seems to me allusively evident from a small detail: the frightening absence of «uniforms and *insignia*», honest guarantees of foreign war, which make possible an immediate response to Schmitt's discriminating question as to «who the enemy is». Now in fact, in the internal war, the question falls into a void, while uniforms and *insignia* have as equivalent no «marque apparent», but only confusion and disorder.

Europe at the end of the sixteenth century was a time of brutal transition: the static humanist peace had already dissolved and the horizon showed not a ray of hope that the cruelty and persecution exercised against one's opponent could be overcome, even temporarily. The first decades of the seventeenth century were a turning point for thought, though no longer a return to the medieval aura of the *justa causa belli*. Instead they paved the way for the classic solution of the modern State, thereby positing the conditions for the monopoly of legitimate violence. But for the moment the problem was the preliminary one of defending oneself and surviving in circumstances of 'disorder', without yet indicating general models of the relativisation of aggression. One must, despite all, live in conflict.

«Monstrous war: others proceed outside, but this one turns against itself and is corroded by its own poison [. . .] It eludes any discipline» (*Essais*, III, XII). Here civil war saw the category of hostility turning into a gauge of social life, a hypothesis supported by a pessimistic anthropology that on several points anticipated that of Hobbes. Internal war as a disease of the body, it was first of all an absence of discipline, a disorderly release of poisons, of «bad humours» that should have been normalised or repressed. A raw realism little by little replaced the interpretive categories of natural law: as for Hugo Friedrich, «what is fitting for the State, for society, for the family, for customs, is not defined by notions of right and wrong, but of order and disorder».[8] In language as in law, «the spirit that designs its own order in the fluid mass of reality sees itself constantly obliged to capitulate before the novelty that surprises it»; therefore, «the wisest thing is to accept this fluid reality».[9]

Accepting the given instance of disorder, the fact that the cards are irremediably «mêlées», means giving up the myth of a general law of nature, an original form that felicitously dismisses the problem of the unintelligible flow of life. On the contrary, for Montaigne, «we no longer know the truth of things; since nothing reaches us that is not falsified and altered by our senses» (*Essais*, II, XII). «There is the name and there is the thing; the name is a voice indicating and signifying the thing; the name is not part of the thing or of its substance; it is an alien bit joined to the thing and outside it» (*Essais*, II, XVI).

The critique of language shows us, otherwise stated, that the world of things (*Sachlichkeit*), the actual site where social relations are produced, remained formally undefined, precisely because it was shot through with the discordant multiplicity of individual events. But it must at once be said that the critical change represented by Montaigne's scepticism was in no way susceptible to romantic interpretation, namely one that tended to overestimate 'indescribable' individualities and to transfigure them idealistically. The combination of scepticism-irrationalism dear to romantic philosophical-political interpretation must, in the case of Montaigne, be split up in order to emphasise the rationalist function of his conventionalism and his sceptical criticism of experience. (The topic seems inadequately treated even by Borkenau, whose studies on these points are otherwise quite acute.)[10]

The sceptical rejection of a «*Systematisierung der Lebenshaltung*» in no way signifies that the problem of order disappeared from the horizon in the formless triumph of non-rationalisable individualities. The rationalisation process did not necessarily postulate the systematisation of the whole, since, in the case of critical scepticism, only a sort of *Rationalisierung der Teile* was admissible, namely an extreme attention to the single contradictory datum and the will to resolve it independently of its inclusion within mythic systems of the whole.

Sceptical criticism was, however, a clarifying element in the process of rationalising social reality. The fact that sceptical criticism called into question man-world and man-society relationships to the point of sometimes doubting their ultimate practicability did not validate negating the prospect of an order, but rather recognising that order could be achieved, overleaping the negative absoluteness of scepticism simply by emptying itself of any content, to the point of reproducing, as mere hypothesis or convention, the bald skeleton of the 'rule of the game'.

Nominalism is in this context a link of paramount importance in the genealogy of conventional order. As Friedrich says, «order [. . .] has no other role than that of being a rule of the game, an expedient in an existence where everything has revealed itself an expedient, an organised contingency».[11] Rule of the game, convention, expedient; these are the terms that summarise the neutralisation of the contents of value expressed by order, subsequent to scepticism. The skeleton of the 'rule of the game' is what remained after the sceptical destruction of objectivity.

As Horkheimer observes, «that sceptical relativism precludes action had already been held against its Greek exponents. They replied that to act there was no need for knowledge and that probability sufficed.»[12] In fact, the theory that emerged purified by the operation of scepticism of any 'aura' of absoluteness and metaphysical universality 'was content' with proceeding relativistically in function of a non-rational interest, lending itself to being used probabilistically within a given historical context, in function of a determined will. Certainly, as Montaigne thought, it did not constitute a 'truth', and so there lacked a cogent reason to compel commitment to it.

The transition to action thus appeared as if truncated by non-calculable contingencies, starting with the mind, as 'immediate perception and reflection, natural need, laws and tradition, skill acquired with practice and traditional knowledge'.[13] It was also the disordered world of desires which was the bad reality that emerged as the unspeakable motor of action, but desire, and the effect of this desire on the collective action of a social class, would have to wait a long time for the 'Hobbes-scandal' to be taken into consideration by political theory. For now, «from obedience and surrender every other virtue is born, as from thought every sin» (*Essais*, II, XII).

3. *Subdivision of spaces.* – From the contraction of desires to the search for an inner space. Disorder must be 'cured' starting with an inaccessible *ubi consistam*, from a place in which criticism develops far from excesses. «Contraction of my desires and intentions, inability to carry on any kind

of business, and my favourite qualities, idleness, frankness» (*Essais*, III, IX).

The metaphor of «arrière boutique» is all this; to the mannerist splitting of the subject there corresponds a subdivision of the metaphysical spatiality of the modern individual into an inner forum and an outer one (*interior sphaera/exterior sphaera*), or a rigid separation between philosophical-moral criticism and political action. «Arrière boutique» is a symbol of the asceticism that 'cures' one of excesses and guides the spirit towards rationalisation. The consequence of the rigorous delimitation of the inner sphere is to allow the parallel development of an outer sphere, opposed and separate, perfectly logicalised. In other words, the delimitation serves the purpose of preventing elements of 'personal' backwardness, irrational evaluations still alive in one's conscience, from interfering with the outer sphere, in which it is the technique of institutions that must dominate free of conflict.

Only the opposition of the inner to counter the public seriousness of the outer will allow the parallel growth of the two spatial areas, within which the modern individual will unfold. As Horkheimer already observed, in the individual's life interiority plays the same role as churches, museums and places of entertainment and leisure in general do in social life. In the bourgeois age cultural spheres are separate from the economy for both the individual and the social totality. The space of the «arrière boutique», in which inner events clearly display themselves in a game, also recalls very closely the image of the *Spiel-Raum*, which Carl Schmitt recognised as characteristic of European Baroque theatre.[14]

In the *Spiel-Raum* a «theatrical game» takes place – which, however, in no way negates the value of external reality. Even in Montaigne the *exterior sphaera*, human life placed in close contact with juridical and political institutions, had its indisputable validity, although the opposition between the two planes continued to subsist: «le Maire et Montaigne ont tousjours esté deux, d'une separation bien claire» (*Essais*, III, X). In other words, the existence of a State and a legal system as a reality located outside of humanity in no way compromised the growth of a bourgeois ethic of 'individuality', provided this remained contingent and founded on hypothetical bases that conceded at its back a glimpse of the structure of the game.

Yet it is true that the phase destined to prevail, at the origins of the political ethics that characterise the modern state, was embodied by the *pactum dominationis*, and that the already evident way towards absolutism condemned to impotence every individualistic tension that strove to redeem political values that had by then been lost. To all effects, as it has been rightly observed, it is true that modern culture, at its seventeenth-century origins, took an elitist stance. «Even the most daring educational programs, or the proposals for religious tolerance that one encounters in this period, never have as their purpose the liberation of *all* humanity.»[15] It was the very social fabric, in other words, that was divided.

Thus it seems to me that there existed a close link, a secret correspondence between this division, which ran through society like a wound, allowing to some but denying to most a prospect of liberation, and the division of the individual into an 'outer' and an 'inner' self. It can certainly be said that the dissociation of the social world was faithfully mirrored by this split which occurred in the individual structure. But behind this statement lay perhaps a greater number of implications, a cluster of subtler reasons that deserve close scrutiny.

What conceptual relationship was established, first of all, between the bourgeois individual's split into an 'outer' and an 'inner' self and his emancipation? Was there only and simply this relationship of mutual exclusion between the two concepts? Did the decline of the Renaissance dream of 'heroic' liberation of the whole society through the efforts of integral humanistic individualities, did the decline of this revolutionary utopia[16] leave behind, in the classes still far from political power, only helplessness and despair? In reality the split, dictated to the nascent modern State by the political relationships of subordination, was also a prerequisite for the rational use of technical know-how. This gigantic tool for transforming the world – true universal *medium* – could be activated exclusively by individualities reduced to their external sphere. It was once again the post-humanistic individual, afflicted by a total 'loss of integrity',[17] who mastered technical know-how, steering it perhaps towards the objective of collective liberation. Was it still possible to maintain, in this sense, the opposition between 'dissociation' and 'emancipation' which we mentioned at the start?

The *ex post* nature of these considerations is clear. Yet it is true that in the early seventeenth century the mechanistic philosophy of science already met these doubled forms of late mannerist consciousness at several points. From Bacon to Mersenne and Descartes, a reflection on technical know-how demonstrated it. But the supreme demonstration lay in the renunciation by the bourgeois philosophy of the time to undertake any kind of «healing by doubling» and a tendency to split off, in the potent figure of the modern State in its *ratio imperii*, the task of developing individualities from that of the conservation of order.

Moreover, the separation between inner and outer can also explain, for example, why in Hobbes there is a separation between external acts and intimate thought, action and mentality[18] traceable ultimately, as we have already mentioned, to a preferential place in the criticism of bourgeois ideology undertaken by contemporary negative thought: the discord between theory and practice. As long as the unitarism and universality of humanist pre-capitalist relationships continued to subsist, «inner and outer did not constitute [. . .] a true contrast, since the visible establishment of the Church held them together. With the relaxing of the ecclesiastical clamp, the rift deepened. In this the reformers were indicative here, liberating conscience from the old Church, but in return they had to resort to the State.» Thus inner and outer, which even in the thought of Luther and Calvin were distinct from each other, «are not in absolute conflict with each other as long as the external institution of the State fulfils its protective function, that is, as long as it is sufficiently dominated by Christian inner space».[19] The kind of split or 'doubling' that occurs in Montaigne was totally different: scepticism produced among the areas of human activity, between inner spaces of thought and outer spaces of practice, a clear-cut opposition that only at a later time, subsequent to the 'bending' on itself of the sceptical conscience and the functional containment of negative thought, could be associated with 'positive' political outcomes, in the conventional acceptance of State order.

4. *Formalisation of exteriority.* – For Charron too there lay at the centre of the entire problem of the perception of ethical-political experience the caesura of modernity and, with it, the crisis that took place in the structure of individual consciences: the loss of 'aura'. It is perhaps from a passage (deeply marked by Montaignian tones) of the second book of *Sagesse* that the Charron question started to be taken into consideration in its exact terms in relation to the problem of the State: «We need to know how to distinguish and separate ourselves from our public offices; each of us plays two roles and two characters, the one a stranger and apparent, the other proper and essential [. . .] We need to use the world as it is, nonetheless considering it as something alien to itself . . .» (*Sagesse*, II, II). Here we see even more clearly that every social organicism, each undisputed synthesis between the individual and his institutions, is indeed excluded from the start, since the individual in his solitude laden with the enormous potential of moral criticism appears completely extraneous and separate from the «great body» of social opinion and from the State.

To better understand the meaning of this separation, which would lead to the typically libertine and mannerist renunciation of any political behaviour, we need to recon-

sider with Lenoble the contrast between the moral phi-
losophies of Charron and Mersenne («deux spiritualités
qui s'opposent radicalement»).[20] Charron, before the voluntarism of a Mersenne, who sees morality as a positive
decree of God, a decree 'posited' in function of the preservation of the existing juridical-political order, upholds
a rational morality as a place of inner freedom, which
produces criteria potentially antagonistic to the positive
order (and therefore rightly considered by Mersenne as
«dangerous»). It should at once be noted that this potential antagonism of reason against the existing order is in
Charron constantly inhibited and led back to interiority,
far from risky political developments and any temptation
to proceed to action: to any real «reform of humanity».[21]

Nothing was more alien for the libertine thread of
seventeenth-century political thought than the 'reform
of humanity': just when, for the bourgeois who counted,
what mattered was, in Marxist terms, solely the reproduc-
tion of his own social existence, such a reform ideal could
only seem a butt of irony.[22] Charron's moral rationalism
was aware of not being able to explain, on the basis of
its own criteria, the intricate phenomenology of political
life: the external, 'demonic' dimension of human life. This
inevitably led to conformism, since «precisely their awareness of the non-rational, "mystical" foundation of the
authority of all that is law, custom and religion induced
the wise not to attempt any criticism of the public sphere,
much less try to subvert it».

Political conformism, which manifested itself in the
public adherence to absolutism, fed for Charron on the
perfectly mannerist recognition of the last characteristics
that mark the foundation of the concept of authority, characteristics defined almost as 'unfathomable'[23] and 'mystical'. There was, in other words, in Charron's mannerism
an intentionally constructed grey area whose purpose was
to mask the true meaning of Charron's thought concerning the problem of the ultimate value which founds every
order of life.[24] This grey area, this assumption that in all of

Charron was omitted, was motivated by the fact that in the aftermath of libertine-mannerist scepticism fundamental value was totally lacking and that, on the other hand, the mere legacy of the past was no longer tolerable: if at all, the preference for such a legacy is a mere defence of the force of what exists, a defence that often ends up performing, in the historical contingency, a positive instrumental function.

Once again the apology of what exists moved hand in hand with complete disenchantment (achieved internally) over the dissolution of values; *foris ut moris, intus ut libet.* What should be clear by now is that this coexistence of opposing elements, defence and disenchantment, is just seemingly paradoxical, given the fact that value, though literally 'dissolved' in a philosophical context, was, in the political one, still admissible on the basis of considerations of concrete opportuneness (*prudence, preud'hommie, sagesse*).

Now the problem was to clothe force in the vestments of legality: to consolidate the State's absolute authority against the centrifugal forces of subjects able as such to pursue only their individual interests. Charron's attempt at an answer reclaimed, as is known, the substance of Montaigne's positivism, anticipating on this point certain convictions that would become Pascal's: laws and customs must be obeyed for their own sake, and not because they are just. These were strictly positivist conceptions which comprised, in an intensified ethical formalism, the entire area of life's phenomena. If the mere formality of a command suffices to instil in the populace the obligation of obedience, then it must be said that the ethics that still continue to subsist on a rational basis, but only in one's inner self, are politically neutralised.

In the game of outward appearances that constituted the sphere of the political in history, ethics ceased to have any value, and for the isolated individual who found himself perchance in contrast with the State there was nothing for it but flight or martyrdom. «*Fugere aut pati,* de troisieme je n'en trouve poinct; l'un de ces remedes est de guerpir, s'enfuyr, quitter le pays et la terre. L'autre de souffrir et endurer toute chose.»[25] This was a typically mannerist aspect of Charron's political philosophy: the inner/outer dialectic, already identified as a genetic instance of the modern split between the private and public spheres, found its deepest meaning in metaphysics, as a split of essence and phenomenal appearance.

It suffices to mention the perspective that this question opened onto the history of ethical-political conventionalism. This perspective can be tentatively summarised as follows: nothing need be said about essence as a place of value, for whoever asserts a value publicly, or transposes into exteriority the issue of the ultimate essence of order, would provoke the spread of disintegrative criticism; vice versa, it must be said of appearance that it harbours the language proper to 'the Political', insofar as it is the language of practical exteriority, or the channel of social communication which shapes values utilitarianly, in view of their external use and estimation (*reductio ad pretium*).

The root of this concept is undoubtedly mannerist, by which the 'apparent' forms of perception are the sole reality, validated and validating, of which history is able to acquire knowledge. Socially objectified forms (market-related institutions on the one hand and State-related ones on the other) are based solely on apparent logic, which is the logic that is proper as much to ethics and economics (in the dual meaning, moral and economic, of the term 'value'), as to the entire area of the law (given the exterior regulatory function characteristic of 'norms'). Market law, the subjectivist mechanisms of supply and demand, comprise the world of value with no remainder, no space that is free from the quantitative determination of interest and utility. Life completely dominates the forms of knowledge.[26] In this setting the concepts of 'pride', 'vanity', etc., fundamental for seventeenth-century political anthropology, came to constitute mere economic forms of evaluation of physical power, for the pursuit of well-being and personal happiness.

The moment this mannerist process of formalisation of sensory appearance reached maturity it showed up in Hobbes, in his disenchanted reduction of the value of man to his price (*Leviathan*, I, X). Only then was the logic of appearance completely formalised and capable of being considered concretely productive of socioeconomic relationships guaranteeing the affirmation of bourgeois individualism.

5. *Convention.* – Hobbes's theory can be compared to the production of so-called «constructive scepticism»),[27] which, as in Mersenne or Gassendi, attenuates only the negative-critical brunt of radical scepticism, affirming the utility or even irreplaceability of conventional hypotheses for the development of mechanistic science. In Hobbes «the arbitrarism attributed to the divinity ended up welding itself seamlessly with the conventionalism of science and the artificiality of civil law, in a renewed interpretation of God, the world and man, by which rationality, far from finding a static mirroring in being, was forced to continually review its conclusions, confronted by a will that for the first time and distinctly hinted at something alien and irreducible to itself».[28] The absolute lack of a natural mirroring between reason and being was the resolutely anti-humanist element that Hobbes derived from the philosophical-political scepticism that went back to Montaigne. But in Hobbes, as opposed to Montaigne, everything became artifice, an empty name that embraced a rigorous logic of vanity and appearance which would find precise textual acknowledgements, in another period of the European crisis, only in Nietzsche's critique.

In both Hobbes and Nietzsche a resolute nominalism covers, in the field of ethics, indifferentistic-nihilistic assessments and assumptions. Logic is that of *pretium* and language is motivated by the mechanics of the passions: now «*ratio* is nothing but *oratio*» and «the passions of man, since they are the first cause of all our voluntary motions, are also the first cause of speech, which is the motion of its tongue» (Hobbes, *Elements*, I, V, 14). The single-minded consideration of authors such as Hobbes and Nietzsche applies itself forcefully to an investigation of the history of concepts, in a careful evaluation of how they represent the complete, perfectly logical and rigorous distortion of humanist scepticism. The world, insofar as we can know it, is nothing but our nervous activity.

Among the passions, vanity has a logical role of central importance: if in Hobbes the value of a man is determined by his price, in Nietzsche «that fundamental conviction, according to which, on the waves of society, we have a good crossing or suffer shipwreck much more for what we are considered than for what we are: a conviction that has to be the helm of any act in relation to society is designated and branded with the extremely generic word "vanity"...»[29] *In exteriore sphaera* the substance of a man is not visible, estimable (reducible to *pretium*): this means that it does not count in the game of convention, that it is not there that the form of 'name' becomes being, the only being possible, the only metaphysical structure effectively in operation. Conventional names and words 'shelter' the subject, are according to what will be Nietzsche's expression, «the skin of the soul».[30] Language as money and vice versa: in Hobbes too there are, as in Nietzsche, «word-coins» and «concept-coins».

The *Elements* are illuminating anticipations, in this sense, of the 'economic' concept of logic that is typical of individual passions such as glory, honour, pride: it suffices to think of the profoundly indicative example provided by the so-called metaphor of racing (Hobbes, *Elements*, I, IX, 21). In it his analysis of passions reaches, even while examining analogous topics explainable only within a radically secularised anthropology, results that are opposed to those of late humanist scepticism, whose stronghold lies in these passages from Montaigne: «few passions have disturbed my sleep; but in regard to decisions, the least one disturbs me. Just as I avoid the slanting, slippery sides of streets, and I take to the middle parts, full of mud and ruts, from which I cannot slide any lower, and will seek the safest place» (*Essais*, II, XVII). In Hobbes's race, we might say, Montaigne is afraid and shrinks: «The fear of a fall upsets me more than a fall itself. The game is not worth the candle» (ibid.).

For Hobbes, on the contrary, honour is the mere recognition of power (*Elements*, I, VIII, 5) and «honour and honesty are merely the same thing in persons of different ranks». As for glory, «whether inner feeling of complacency or triumph of the mind, it is the passion that derives from the imagination or concept of our power, superior to the power of him who opposes us [. . .]; this passion is called pride by those who are jarred by it: but by those for whom it is welcome, it is called a proper sense of self-worth» (*Elements*, I, IX, 1).

In the eyes of the nihilistic technique «of appearance», delineated in a nominalist key by the Hobbes-Nietzsche line, the domain of artificiality must be total: nature is never the opposite good, the reassuring and liveable model to which existence should be made to return. Convention allows for the full acceptance of the inhuman, of man reduced to a body moving in space, far from any classical perspective of natural law. Hobbes, or at least a certain Hobbes, might be the author of passages such as this:

> Will you live according to nature? O noble Stoics, what an imposture of words! Picture a being like nature, wasteful beyond measure, indifferent beyond measure, without intentions and concerns, without mercy and justice, fecund and squalid and at the same time insecure, picture indifference itself as power; how could you live according to such indifference? Is living not precisely a desire to be different from what nature is? Is living not evaluating, preferring, being unjust, being limited, wanting to be different?» (Nietzsche, *Beyond Good and Evil*, 13)

Libertines knew all this, and from here Hobbes undertook his fight against the dreadful indifference of nature, seen as a desert where man can only die brutally. In nature there is no justice, and therefore neither is there injustice (Hobbes, *De cive*, I, X): which is just a seeming paradox. A way out of this nightmare imposes itself, and this way leads necessarily to the Leviathan, the great machine, whose power to make just what is unjust is welcomed by those who live in deadly indifference of nature, as the providential advent of a kingdom in which univocal distinctions are at last in force.

This escape from the state of nature, in introducing a completely new source of meaning and legitimacy, contributed to formulate an unprecedented metaphor: «The divine character of "sovereign", "omnipotent" state power does not consist here in a foundation understood as a theoretical argument. The sovereign is not the *Defensor Pacis* of a peace that leads back to God; he is a creator of a peace that is nothing but earthly, this Creator of Peace.»[31] This creation from nothing is a constant of decisionist thought: the image of *tabula rasa* as primordial situation, only starting from which can the decision be made, leads back to the concept of Hans Blumenberg's «absolute metaphor».[32]

It is hard to say whether this concept, with all that it implies, can apply adequately to Hobbes's concept. What is certain is that the metaphor of creation *ex nihilo*, understood as the inconceivability of an order that is prior to the decision, opens the way to distinguishing, with Schmitt, a perfect decisionism (the 'classic' Hobbesian one) from an imperfect one:

In fact, before the disappearance of the ancient and Christian conceptions concerning the order of the world, replaced by the new natural scientific thought, thought was firmly dominated by concepts inherent to order as a presupposition of decision. As such, the idea that nothing else existed before decision was already preliminarily limited and relativised by the idea of order. Decision itself became the expression of a presupposed order. When the jurist and theologian Tertullian says: 'We are obliged to something not because it is good, but because God commands it' ('neque enim quia est bonum, idcirco auscultate debemus, sed quia Deus praecipit'), this expression already sounds like juridical decisionism; but because of the Christian concept of God as still presupposition in Tertullian's thought, there is still lacking here the conscious idea of a total disorder, one that can be transformed into law and order not by means of a rule, but only thanks to a simple decision.[33]

We can then say that Hobbes's sovereign, a mortal God, not only ensures, as in Cartesian-occasionalist philosophy, the correspondence between name and thing, but determines it actively, in a sense very close to Blumenberg's of the creation of an absolute metaphor. Thus the power of one who wields sovereignty over 'names' and over language as effective dispenser of arbitrary values imposes itself universally as conventional logic.

The destruction of any ontology entails the negation of a concept of truth that is unbound from the context of life. Knowing is exercising power and, tendentially, a will. Only Nietzsche, starting from these premises, would carry out a critique of logic based on the concrete interests of life: for him, «the question remains open: are logical axioms adequate for reality or are they the criteria and means for creating reality, the concept of "reality" for us? [. . .] To be able to state the first requires [. . .] already knowing being: which is absolutely not the case. Therefore the principle does not contain a criterion of truth, but an imperative about what should count as true. [. . .] In reality, logic (such as geometry and arithmetic) applies only to fictitious truths, which have been created by us. Logic is the attempt to understand, or better, to render formulable, calculable for us, according to a scheme of being put in place by us, the real world.»[34] Ethical relativism thus presupposes a

Corollary I

radical theoretical nihilism, whose logic is contained and faithfully reproduced in the jurisprudence of political power.

Corollary II
The Problem of a Political Theology

1. *First definitions.* – We may say, as an initial, broader approximation, that political theology poses the problem of the relationships between the dimension of 'political' and the transcendent *Veritas*. In Hobbes – as Schmitt's interpretation claims[1] – allowance is given (or even postulated) for an exceptional 'opening' of the political system towards the *Veritas* revealed in Scripture.

> The truth that *Jesus is the Christ* that Hobbes proclaimed so often and so clearly as his own faith and conviction, is a truth of public faith, of *public reason* and of public worship in which each citizen takes part. In Hobbes's mouth it does not sound at all like a simple tactical statement, as an instrumental lie dictated by the need to protect himself from prosecution and censorship. It is also something different from the *moral par provision* by which Descartes adhered to the traditional faith. In the transparent construction of the political system of the *Matter, Form and Power of a Commonwealth ecclesiastical and civil,* that truth is actually the closing element, and the expression *Jesus is the Christ* calls by name the God present in public worship. The frightful civil war of the Christian sects raised at once the problem of who should interpret and perfect in a legally binding way that truth which gradually needs to be interpreted? Who decides what true Christianity is? Is it the inevitable *Quis interpretabitur?* of the unsuppressible *Quis iudicabit?* Who coins truth in legal tender? To this problem the maxim responds: '*Auctoritas, non*

veritas facit legem'. Truth is not accomplished by itself, but needs coercible commands. To bring this about a *potestas directa* is called upon, which – unlike a *potestas indirecta* – is the implementation of the command, obtaining obedience and able to defend those who obey it. In this way a chain is created from top to bottom, from the truth of public worship to obedience and to the protection of the individual. If we start instead from the bottom and not from the top, that is from the system of the material needs of the individual, then the chain starts from the need for protection and security of the individual, 'by nature' in need of advice and help, and by the obedience that follows, and leads along the same path but in a reversed sequence, to the door open onto transcendence.[2]

The system of material needs – which finds its clearest 'political' expression in the need to obey in order to obtain protection – while being inspired by a rigorous, autonomous logic, does not play itself out on that level, i.e. does not remain a closed, unrelated entity, but is forcibly in contact with a different level of meaning. *Veritas* makes up the core of the 'theological': the point which marks the full development of the *Sinnfrage* of life's multiple systems. Between 'theological' and 'political' dimension there is analogy, *imitatio*,[3] but not only (and not so much) in the sense of a theologising of politics, or of a movement from top to bottom from *Veritas* to *Auctoritas*, but also (and above all) in the sense of a politicisation of theology, where *Auctoritas*, by means of an omnipotent interpretation, may even succeed in overturning the initial meaning of *Veritas* (and of natural law), its letter.

The logic of the political becomes the hermeneutics of *Veritas*, but in the very special sense by which the latter – at one time seen *sub specie politica* – ceases to exist as such in order to appear filtered into the language of *Auctoritas*. *Veritas* provides content, *Auctoritas* the form of decision, but the contents after the decision are no longer the same.[4]

Only a second source of sovereignty, a *potestas indirecta*, could repropose them by means of a new, different inter-pretation, but precisely for this reason a *potestas indirecta* is firmly challenged in Hobbes's system.

In a desire to take stock of what has been said so far, we can – I think – distinguish between three different seman-tic levels of the concept of political theology, which we shall designate with the exponents 1, 2 and 3:

political theology[1]: (politicisation of the theological) is the theology of (i.e. subjective genitive) political power, or the concept of truth which is held by the sovereign of the moment.

political theology[2]: (theologisation of the political) is the theology of (i.e. objective genitive) political power, or what theology says about the nature of political power.

political theology[3]: is the theory of transformation (*Umbesetzung*), based on the principle of analogy, of theo-logical concepts reformulated as legal concepts (especially constitutional law and the doctrine of the State) and politi-cal ones.

It is clear that Schmitt's idea of the concept is much closer to the meaning of the first level than to the second. More precisely: the political theology concept is employed in several contexts in the first sense, while it is never interpretable *only* in the second. As for the third level, it is undoubtedly always present in Schmitt's analysis, but nonetheless it seems incapable of exhausting the political theology concept: it is exact but partial.[5]

2. *The ultimate foundation of legitimacy in politics.* – Political theology, in its three levels identified so far, is seemingly compatible only with a one-tier model of representation of power. Monarchy and monotheism, as 'pure' forms of the manifestation of will, are the indispensable background of analysis, supported by the assumption that «the purer the will, the more certain the command and the greater the order».[6] It is a theory of politics that believes itself capable of bringing all forms of social and political pluralism to a

clearer conceptualisation, to the point of decisively subli-
mating the characters in the figure of the organism. The
latter eliminates the *pluriversum* and exposes the indivis-
ible root of sovereignty. In this sense:

> The term 'sovereignty' is used here in a positive sense,
> like the term 'unity'. Neither of the two means that
> every single moment of the existence of every person
> who is part of a political unity is to be determined
> and controlled by the 'political', or that a centralised
> system should cancel out every other organisation or
> constituency. It may be that economic considerations
> are stronger than any will of the government of any
> State which claims to be neutral in economic matters;
> in the same way the power of a State which claims
> to be neutral in religious matters is in any case easily
> limited in religious convictions. What counts always
> are solely instances of conflict. If the economic, cultural
> or religious counterforces are so strong as to determine
> by themselves alone the decision in a critical case, this
> means that they have become the new substance of
> political unity.[7]

The classic problem of a theory of the legitimacy of
juridical-political systems is dealt with, from this point of
view, in a rather special way: political theology does not so
much attempt to assert the sacredness of authority[8] as to
reconnect itself, in terms of the history of political theories,
to certain presuppositions already implicit in the doctrine
of divine right (e.g. the metaphysical primacy of monar-
chic form)[9] or in any case of the claim of the *personalistic
phase* in the proceedings of government: «In any transformation an *auctoritatis interpositio* is present.»[10]

Which results, in the era in which «there are no longer
kings» (Donoso Cortés), in a necessary inclination towards
the principle of dictatorship, as an element for resolving
key policy decisions in the context of modern mass democracies. It should be remembered that

The natural form of the immediate expression of the will of a people is the voice that consents or denies the *acclamatio* to the assembled crowd. In large modern States acclamation, which is a natural, necessary manifestation of the life of any people, has changed its form. Here it is manifested as 'public opinion' [. . .]. But in general a people can always say either yes or no, assent or deny, and its yes or no is all the more simple and elementary the more it is a fundamental decision regarding their existence as a people.[11]

It would be useful at this point, also in light of this passage, to propose a fourth semantic level of the concept of political theology, which in the context of the considerations developed so far seems the most interesting and comprehensive:

political theology[4]: the general concept of the ultimate foundation of legitimacy in politics. The theory of legitimacy is seen here as a form of knowledge aimed at the ultimate relationship which exists between 'political' and *Veritas*.

Below I will try to verify its centrality as Schmitt understands (but not only) this semantic level.

3. *The metaphysical presuppositions of nihilist theology. Jus reformandi or* jus revolutionis. – One of the main theological-political problems, perceived as such by constitutional and State doctrine, undoubtedly lies in the construction of an «image of mankind» (*Menschenbild*).[12] It is a problem deriving from the developments of classical philosophical anthropology, whose formulation lies in the question of whether an infinite transformation of human nature is possible by means of the 'political'.

It is doubtless possible today, technically, to modify on a planetary scale the levels of consciousness and life of huge masses. The reality of «collective man» as a labour machine concedes by now precious little to the Marxist optimism of the *Grundrisse*.[13] This holds true everywhere: the progressive narrowing of the spaces of individuality is not just a trend of totalitarian regimes.

Nihilism is not an ideological option, a subjective choice on the part of individuals or social collectivities: it is an objective tendency, a compelling presence (even if at times dismissed) over the forms of Western thought. Decisively detaching the dimension of the 'theological' from that of the 'political', denying – as does Ernst Bloch,[14] and with him, Walter Benjamin[15] – that the ranks of the profane can forge a link with or mimic the kingdom of God, has the effect of denying the feasibility of any strategy of resistance of individuals for stopping (or at least delaying, in the terms of St Paul's *katechon*)[16] the advent of Apocalypse.

And in this case it is certainly not a question of lumping together, without further distinctions, Schmitt and Benjamin in what is «the religion of atheists, the politics»:[17] the metapolitical Schmitt proceeds, on the contrary, in the context of Weber's late polemic against the technicistic neutralisation of struggle among values, to hypothesise the providential growth – as a force of renewal within the technicist-totalitarian organism – of «new elites growing out of asceticism and a more or less voluntary poverty, a poverty that signifies above all rejection of the security afforded by the *status quo*».[18]

In Benjamin, on the other hand, the dissolving of the link between the ranks of the profane and the kingdom of God is carried out with extreme rigour. No synthesis exists, because «what is historical» can never rise to the messianic dimension, nor is the Justice-God in any way referable to the Love-God.[19]

The reconciliation of these two poles, implicit in the Catholic 'symbol', enters into conflict with the Judaic idea of the remoteness of the Messiah, the 'not-yet-come'. As has been keenly observed, «Benjamin, who exacerbates the perspective of Judaic messianism, understands the advent of the Kingdom in terms of theocracy, a dimension of government and power, a non-eschatological liberation of the People [. . .] Benjamin's Judaism therefore favors blurring the distinction between theology and theocracy»,[20] with the result of making practicable only an atheistic perspective to those who feel, with justice, obliged to rebel against the theocratic implications of theology.

This atheistic perspective involves legitimating the *jus revolutionis* as a fundamental principle of political and, inseparably, theological transformation. *Jus revolutionis* expresses a profound tension towards the absolute *novum*, in the sense Hans Blumenberg uses,[21] and posits itself as an exact counterpart of *jus reformandi*, which is instead strictly related to the concept – formulated by Schmitt in *Politische Theologie II* – of *Umbesetzung*, a slow process of secularising-detheologising of religious formats to a *Struktur-Verwandtschaft* placeable in the theoretical context of Scheler's sociology of knowledge.[22] A process not without repercussions regarding the political theory of conflict and its momentary juridical-state discontinuance. According to Schmitt, «the religious civil wars of the sixteenth and seventeenth century Reformation era hinged on the *jus reformandi* of the Christian Church; they regarded internal theological controversies, at times internal Christological ones. Hobbes's *Leviathan* was the result of a specifically theological-political period. An age of *jus revolutionis* and total secularisation was to follow.»[23]

Would political theology (especially political theology[3] and political theology[4]) then be a form of knowledge adequate for posing as its object the problems of *Umbesetzung* and *Struktur-Verwandschaft*? Some points of *Politische Theologie II* help us give a positive answer to this question.

4. *Legitimacy vs legality. The so-called «need for legitimacy».* – «My work on political theology» – says Schmitt – «does not move as part of some widespread metaphysics, but concerns the classic case of a transformation (*Umbesetzung*) that takes place with the help of specific concepts, which have emerged in the context of systematic thought about both of the historically most advanced structures of Western

rationalism, namely the Catholic Church, with its juridical rationality, and the State of *jus publicum Europaeum*, which in Hobbes' system is still thought of as Christian.»[24] The reality of such an *Umbesetzung* is indeed a 'classic case' and forms a central field of the historical-juridical knowledge which – as Schmitt repeatedly emphasises – should not be downstaged by scientific methods based on the principle of legality hurled as a weapon against that of legitimacy.

Theology and jurisprudence not only operate, for Schmitt, «*mit strukturell-kompatiblen Begriffen*»,[25] but have by now created, through their interactions, complex contexts «between which even enharmonic exchanges become admissible and full of meaning».[26] These contexts are starting to be analyzed only by expanding the area of scientific methodology to encompass the problem of the relationship with transcendent *Veritas*. Such a positive relationship with *Veritas* – Schmitt argues against restrictive positivist methodologies – may be viable: «it is just a matter of being able to fine-temper the tools».[27]

We have just said: modern scientific methodologies hurl the principle of legality as a weapon against that of legitimacy. This concept needs to be looked into, in a way suggested in a short but pregnant passage of *Das Problem der Legalität*:

The transformation of law into legality is a consequence of positivism: an inevitable consequence as soon as a political system differentiates itself from the Church. From the sociological standpoint it is part of the development of the late-industrial era. From the standpoint of the history of philosophy *it is part of the transformation of thought focused on substance into thought focused on function*: a transformation that, until recently, had been *touted as a milestone of scientific and cultural progress*. The preoccupying picture that results from an incessant functionalisation of humanity has been admirably illustrated, even recently, by Serge Maiwald in his Tübingen review 'Universitas'. But already more than thirty years ago, a great German sociologist, Max Weber, had correctly pronounced the diagnosis and its related prognosis.[28]

The principle of legality thus produces the effect of neutralising any reference to the issue of value. Legality versus legitimacy, administration versus value, *novum* versus *Umbesetzung*, *Subjektive Werte* versus *Seins-Werte*: these are the terms of the attack moved aggressively on the field of scientific methodology, by positivism *lato sensu* against any residual dimension of metapolitics. Auguste Comte would recognise in this «an additional argument for his thesis, according to which the canonist replaces the lawyer as, in the past, the theologian the metaphysician». Where he however notes that «from Comte onwards we had many new experiences regarding the irrepressible need for legitimation (*Legitimierungsbedürfnis*) that is inherent in every man».[29]

This inexhaustible «need for legitimacy» has the effect of leading back to Scheler's thematic series on objective value, the shrewd scientific methodologies born from the scepticism of Kantian criticism. Even in a world demythicised and «devoid of prophecy» (in Weber's sense of *Wissenschaft als Beruf*) there persists, as strong as ever, the tension at the overreaching of a merely formalist-conventionalist ethic.[30] And one can flee the 'tyranny' exerted by subjective values, their explicit arbitrarism: *a) in interiore homine*, carefully reconsidering the classic themes of ontology, which reaffirm themselves as unavoidable (we recall Heidegger's prognosis of the *Unverborgenheit* of Being);[31] *b*) at the institutional level, by still seriously considering the possibility of *an effective political myth*, which acts at the level of social psychology to orient society towards revised models of community.

5. *Theological-political objectivism?* – It is not a question of evoking non-conflictual political theories. The 'political' is dominated by conflict, and a dismissal of this by means of powerful ideological mechanisms seems unthinkable.

The peace granted will never be a *pax vera*, but only a *pax apparens*. Nevertheless, a political myth, to be effective, must sustain as true this *pax apparens*. The symbol of the *existenzielle Ordnung* testifies to this profound need to anchor the 'political' to a metapolitics which does not neglect the mythical aspect emerging from every dimension of meaning.

Those who signal the «expediential» nature of Schmitt's recourse to the concepts of theology, «borrowing them» to justify his concept of the political,[32] may have a point, but this criticism reveals itself on close inspection as superficial, since it fails to consider the reasons that determine the intimate logical necessity of this «borrowing». Against the dissolutive aggression of subjective mass values, against self-authorisation (*Selbstermächtigung*) extended to any subject in a mass context of the right to valuations, behaviour and judgements initially permitted only in a narrow context, uncrossable if not at the cost of upsetting the balance of order, the choice of the brake, the *Aufhalter*, the *katechon*,[33] is 'politics' in the strong sense. It is the condition of possibility (the «external support», *Außenhalt*, in Roman Schnur's felicitous expression) for the development of each cultivated interiority, saved from the inevitably bloody outcomes of conflict and destined to circumscribed spaces unreached by the *Weltbürgerkrieg*.

6. *Some concluding theses and a final doubt.* – We can now try to formulate briefly, from what has been said so far, some theses about the nature of political theology. These make no claim to reach definitive conceptual results, or even substantial or methodological ones, about so vast and elusive a subject as that – undertaken from the start – of the relationship between the dimension of the 'political' and transcendent *Veritas* (this latter understood in the meaning it has in Hobbes's lexicon). What we are after is instead some additional argument in favour of the theoretical legitimacy of political theology (especially political theology[4] and political theology[3]) as a form of knowledge adequate for analysing such an area of relationships.

1) The 'political' demands a positive relationship with the 'theological': a relationship that enables us to thematise knowledgeably the area of symbolic meanings that revolve around sacrality, delimiting their impact of violence. If it is true, as for Girard, that «the procedures which enable people to moderate their violence are all alike, since no one is a stranger to violence», and if it is also true that «there is reason to believe that they are all rooted in the religious experience», in whose context «the judicial system refers to a theology that guarantees the truth of its justice»,[34] then the political-theological context provides irreplaceable investigative elements for understanding the symbolism that presides over the social legitimacy of its systems.

Scientific understanding of the 'political' – contrarily to what is required by the positivistic approach, to which a scientific methodology has been erroneously attributed – demands that a positive connection of meaning be established with the 'theological', not only because the problems of power and government necessarily involve *res mixtae*, but also because it is now clear that the question of the symbolic legitimacy of its systems has become once again all the more pressing in the post-industrial civilisation dominated by socio-political sub-systems and by the fragmentation of interest groups, which weave a network of effective (esoteric) power beneath the formal-juridical representations of valid (exoteric) power, whose most visible icons are the rule of law and democracy. But the very idea of democracy (like that – only negative-procedural – of the rule of law) does not escape being made the subject of theological-political investigation.

It might even be said that:

2) Positing democracy as the supreme value is also a postulate of political theology (p.th.[4]). As Schmitt observes:

> On a theoretical level – and in critical times also a practical one – democracy appears powerless against the Jacobin argument, i.e., against the decisive identification of a minority with the entire people and against

the passage of the concept itself from the quantitative sphere to the qualitative one. Our interest now turns to the activity of construction and formation of the popular will, and *the faith that all power comes from the people contains in itself a meaning analogous to the belief that every supreme power comes from God.* These two propositions allow us on the level of political achievements various solutions of government and leave open numerous juridical consequences. *A scientific treatment of democracy must refer to that particular field of study which I have designated by the name of political theology.* Since in the nineteenth century parliamentarism and democracy were concepts linked together to such a degree as to be almost equivalent, these observations on democracy ended up being ignored. We must nevertheless consider that there may well exist at any moment a democracy devoid of modern parliamentarism and a parliamentarism devoid of democracy. Similarly, dictatorship is as little the opposite of democracy as democracy is of dictatorship.[35]

At the beginning of § 2 I said that «apparently» political theology is only compatible with a one-tier model of representation of power. I can now state that it (and in particular p. th.[4]) does not cease being meaningful where the historical-spiritual forms of monarchy and monotheism have been obscured. The validity of a political-theological knowledge continues to exist unchanged in the social and cultural *pluriversum* of the present, since it stems from the timeless problem of *political unity*. In democracies there develops more forcefully the problematic nature of the concept of «political unity», since the bond uniting its members is weaker than that of integral communities.[36]

The fundamental concept of «political unity» should not, however, be hypostatised: it arises from conflict and is 'born again' in conflict. The philosophy of history behind such a concept of «political unity» can never simply amount to a doctrine of «world harmony»,[37] but rather to a Christological doctrine,[38] which presents a serious reconsideration of the possibility of 'worldly' salvation from the disorder (also political) that followed the fall. What occurs, however, is the irrevocable loss – in the context of a political theology – of the serene *Stimmung*, far from the idea of a 'radical evil', which pervades the sixteenth-century passage from John Donne cited by Spitzer:

> God made this whole world in such an uniformity, such a *correspondency*, such a *concinnity* of parts that it was an *Instrument, perfectly in tune*: we may say, the trebles, the highest strings were desordered first; the best understandings, angels and men, put this instrument *out of tune*. God rectified all again, by putting in a *new string*, *semen mulieris*, the seed of the woman, the Messias: And onely by sounding that string in your ears, become we *musicum carmen*, true *musick*, true *harmony*, true peace to you.[39]

3) A political theology (political theology[4], but also [3] and [1]) seems linked instead to a doctrine of the 'harmony of irregularity': in the sense attributed with exactitude by Mersenne to this espression.[40] As Schnur observes on this point,

> Mersenne's thought [. . .] expressed the ultimate impossibility, in the world, a truly 'harmonic' regularity, which appeared literally submerged by wholly irreconcilable contradictions. In this context Mersenne drew on the idea of a 'harmony of irregularity', the concept that perceived a secret harmony behind empirically observable irregularity [. . .]. [All this] evaded public discussion and recognition by the masses, with the result that only the 'wise' were given the task of revealing the true meaning of 'the harmony of irregularity' and of indicating it to the sovereign.[41]

This ultimate allusion to the sovereign once again confirms the even practical function of political theology (especially political theology[4] and [1]) among the «sciences of advisors to the State»: starting with conflict, the task is to restore order through a realistic acceptance of the end of the «unified field» of meanings (Spitzer).

The story of how this unified field (harmony of the world – tempered balance) ceased to exist is none other than the history of modern civilisation; of Weber's '*Entzauberung der Welt*' or de-Christianisation; and our investigation shows us that it is necessary to re-structure Western history. The destruction of the homogeneous 'field' began during the seventeenth century and was completed in the eighteenth. It was this period, and not the Renaissance, that enacted the great hiatus of Western history; in effect we must contrast the two periods, pagan antiquity and Christianity [. . .], with the era of de-Christianisation (from the seventeenth century onwards), in which our field was radically destroyed. At the end of the eighteenth century, the word *Stimmung* crystallised, by then devoid of its lush vitality. We cannot err by attributing this effect to the Enlightenment spirit, the mortifying act which was so well illustrated by Novalis in his treatise *Christenheit oder Europe* (1798); and it is significant that that historian of Europeanism (which he identified with Christianity), who advocated a return to the *heiliger Sinn* (the sense of the divine), in narrating how the Reformation and the Enlightenment had destroyed medieval piety, referred precisely to the *musica mundana* that the mechanistic modern spirit had destroyed:

The hatred which at first was turned especially against the Catholic faith became little by little hatred against the Bible, against the Christian faith, and finally against religion. Moreover the hatred of religion extended, as was logical and natural, to all objects of enthusiasm, banned imagination and sentiment, morality and love of art, the future and the past; subjected mankind, as it did all other natural beings, to necessity and changed the infinite creative music of the universe into the uniform creaking of a monstrous mill, driven by the current of chance and afloat on it, *a mill unto itself, without architect or miller*, and a perfect perpetuum mobile, a mill that grinds up itself (*Novalis' Schriften*, ed. Kluckhohn und Samuel, Leipzig 1929, p. 75).[42]

However, the recovery of a «unified field» of meanings remains an end – a «regulatory idea» in the Kantian sense – which cannot fail to inspire the behaviour of those able to recognise that the problem of truth is something incommensurable and irreducible to the «assemblearist» logic of subjective values. Relativism, as modernity's dominant epistemological approach, reveals here its most glaring limitations.

4) A political theology implies in general a serious reconsideration of what Scheler has to say about «material ethics» and overcoming the arbitrarism arising from the confrontation-clash among mere subjective values.

In his *Tyrannei der Werte*[43] Schmitt examines this complex problem and his customary anti-liberal criticism pits itself critically and controversially against Scheler's, it too aimed against the 'invasion' of subjectivism. The question Schmitt poses at the end of his *Politische Theologie II*, beyond the strong polemic that divides the two authors regarding the theoretical configuration of value, seems to set out from common premises: «Which of the following three freedoms contains the highest degree of aggressiveness: scientific freedom, technical-industrial production, or the choice of free human consumption?»[44]

Each of these freedoms certainly contains the embryo of an uncontrolled development. There remains the serious problem of defining concretely what force can nowadays check mankind's self-authorisation to commit *any* sort of behaviour. There is no use denying that the most clear-cut and at the same time realistic answer to this question has long been: no force, no *Auctoritas*. The regulatory space for the political theology of the Judeo-Christian cultural tradition has thus, in all probability, philosophically speaking, come to an end.

Corollary III

Rhetoric of Ethical Universalism: Jürgen Habermas and the Dissolution of Political Realism

Today there is in vogue a humanitarian religion that regulates the expression of people's thoughts, and if by chance someone defies it, he seems monstrous, just as in the Middle Ages anyone denying the divinity of Jesus would have seemed monstrous.

(V. Pareto, *Cours de sociologie générale*, § 1172, 1)

Die Menschheit entsteht durch Propaganda.

(G. Benn, *Der Ptolemäer. Lotosland*)

1. *A 'civitas maxima' of progress?* – That the *civitas maxima* progress promised by Kant and Kantian idealists reveals itself today, in the phase of multi-ethnic coexistence that is supposed to herald its concrete realisation, a formless, degraded *civitas*, is a paradox that deserves attention. There is in it perhaps a kind of necessity, caused surely by the programmatic disparity that, at least for those still lingering within the Kantian viewpoint, exists between what is and what ought to be, between theoretical dimension and historicity – but caused, further back, by the very nature of the juridical means invoked in order to ensure the success of the pan-communicative cosmopolis. I refer, in the terms Habermas uses, to the so-called law as universal *medium*, or «category of social mediation between facts and norms»:[1] a law that claims contradictorily to embody a certain moral content and simultaneously to remain a neutral technique of communication. This while

it is by now clear – especially in light of recent international events, marked by the experience of 'humanitarian' wars and the widespread, uncontrolled problem of mass immigration – that the *liberal* dream of identifying law (with its inseparable centralised jurisdiction) as the universal means of resolving conflicts corresponds to an abstract normative ideal that does not stand up to criticism stemming from any serious, realistic investigation.

Nevertheless, the temptation to produce facile neutralisations (carefully dissembling the ideological manipulations that from time to time are put in place) continues to be strong and to show up even within theorisations that claim to be a rational response to the logic of violence that inspires the technostructures of global power. This is certainly so in regard to Jürgen Habermas's theory of communicative action, which despite its stated intentions ends up substantially reinforcing the rationales of already strong powers, and therefore lining with cosmopolitan-humanitarian justifications the extreme developments of a doctrine of the intimately coercive costitutional-liberal State. But it is also true that this project does not always succeed in obtaining the desired results for those who conceived it. And this – I would tend to believe – is fortunate for everyone concerned, since in a hypothetical appraisal the damage caused by the extension to a cosmopolis, through the juridical *medium*, of alleged universal ethical models would certainly outweigh the goals of civility that this path ensures.

In this paper I examine some texts, in my view highly questionable, in which Habermas – starting with topics developed in his more or less recent major theoretical works, such as *Theorie des kommunikativen Handelns* (1981) and *Faktizität und Geltung* (1992) – argues in favour of a cosmopolitical law. And he does so in relation to the above-mentioned concrete problems, i.e.: *a*) a universalistic moral content incorporated into law as *medium*; *b*) completion of the historical-cultural enlightenment project through the judicial but perhaps also military imposition of the ideology of human rights. The two topics are obviously intertwined. Their contextual discussion will allow me to better clarify the standpoint, openly alternative to that of Habermas, from which my criticism moves.

2. *Habermas's arguments.* – It is clear that for Habermas law serves essentially as a *medium* for the institutionalising of claims originating in a moral rationalism. Large sections of *Faktizität und Geltung* (but even further back, exemplarily, the conclusive considerations of his *Theorie des kommunikativen Handelns*) are devoted to illustrating what is seen as the fundamental function, exercised by law, of reinforcing the morality of reason (*Vernunftmoral*). «My argument» – Habermas maintains – «is that legal rules and moral norms, after having been *simultaneously* differentiated from traditional ethics [. . .] develop in *parallel* as two different types of rules of action, which yet are able to integrate with each other.»[2]

This should not, however, authorise the revival of classical natural law thought patterns: as Habermas takes pains to clarify:

this reference to morality should not induce us to subordinate law to morality in the sense of a hierarchy of norms. The idea of a 'hierarchy of sources' belongs to the pre-modern world of law. Rather, autonomous morality on the one hand and positive law on the other are arranged in a complementary relationship.[3]

Now, the theoretical topic that best exemplifies this view of the complementarity of law and morality is no doubt that of human rights: a topic that by no accident plays a central role in the late-Enlightenment project of refurbishing the Kantian idea of cosmopolitical law.[4] Human rights, despite their purely moral content, would seem for Habermas to possess, on an equal footing with actual subjective rights, a logical structure suitable for receiving positive satisfaction in a system of binding norms.

But on this point many doubts could in truth issue

forth, especially about the argument advanced in some of Habermas's recent essays, where he addresses – without evading, it would seem, a comparison with strongly divergent theoretical positions – the problem of the practical consequences of his own conception of human rights as a universal source of legitimacy. And yet sooner, of modern law as a rational means of neutralising conflict, placed in close connection with the principles of Kant's morality based on reason, which defines itself as evident.[5]

First, his evaluative premise, which underpins the Kantian project of re-actualisation of the idea of cosmopolitan law, appears thoroughly postulatory. When he states that «in any case, the moral universalism that guided Kant's endeavor remains the fundamental intuition capable of establishing the guiding criteria»,[6] Habermas seems to overlook the fact that this practical-moral self-comprehension of modernity is not the only one possible, and that in any case the intention, proclaimed by any historical force, to 'represent' the interests or the universal value of humanity as a 'whole', seems hypocritical.

In truth, as we can easily learn from the lesson of political realism, «*wer Menschheit sagt, will betrügen*», or: anyone who speaks of humanity is out to deceive. This consideration, far from being, as Habermas would like, a «cloying shred of German ideology» (1998, p. 181) manages to demonstrate adequately how the very intention of juridical globalism – to achieve humanity's moral unity, unified under a single law and a single jurisdiction – conceals a desire to eliminate the discriminatory question of 'who' should actually administer the tenets of such a religion of a unified humanity by assuming the additional power resulting from reinforced legitimacy, put in place in the facile terms of an ethic of (good) intentions. Whoever is called materially to officiate the rites of the religion of human rights ends up actually *deciding* on the concrete allocation of power, in the form of 'rights', in the various spatial spheres in which the universal is necessarily subdivided.

This wilful blindness to the element of decision, sublimated into a neutralising ethics of discourse, has always been one of the weaker points of Habermas's theoretical construct, to the point of arousing the criticism of careful (and unbiased) observers, who have an easy time identifying the specifically deficient aspect of his theory of communicative action in the fact that

> it ignores the problem of the relationship between language and power, the problem of who decides on the rules of language and the modes of formation of interpersonal and social communication [. . .] The function of abstract law and formal equality lies in being the historical forms in which a *power* is structured. Therefore one cannot request of this law [even in the form of human rights and 'cosmopolitical law', *E. C.*] a universal truth whose assertion would require the system to negate itself. Negate that is the *original* (constituent) *decision* that generated it by establishing the distinction between positive law and natural law, between law as social technique and law as measure of reciprocity.[7]

The relevancy of Hobbes's question *Quis iudicabit? Quis interpretabitur?* – as I said – thus returns. A supranational potency, a world «superstate»,[8] or perhaps a universal court of justice?[9] Whatever the answer, Carl Schmitt's observation remains valid: if a historical subject, who necessarily is a stakeholder among other stakeholders, intends to impose on other subjects or peoples certain values *in the name of humanity*:

> his is not a war about humanity, but a war for which a given force seeks to take possession, against his opponent, of a universal concept in order to identify himself with it at the expense of his enemy, in the same way that one can use the concepts of peace, justice, progress and civilisation wrongly, to claim them for oneself and snatch them from one's enemy. 'Humanity' is [in fact] a particularly efficient tool of imperialist expansions [. . .]

By now we know the secret law of this vocabulary and are aware that today the most terrible war can only be undertaken in the name of peace, and the most abject inhumanity only in the name of humanity.[10]

In any case, Habermas implicitly recognises the centrality of Schmitt's critique, when in the same text[11] he expresses – or rather makes a show of expressing – a desire to undertake an analysis of it. And he does so correctly at first in identifying two premises from which this criticism proceeds, summarisable in the following thesis: *a)* the politics of human rights serves the purpose of laying down rules that are part of a *universalistic morality*; *b)* since moral judgements obey a 'good/bad' code, any negative moral evaluation of one's opponent *destroys* the possibility of applying a *juridical-institutional limit* to the political conflict that opposes it.[12]

Habermas intends to counter these two theses, in which he recognises the logical premises of Schmitt's overall critique, by referring to his own conception of the aforementioned complementary relationship of morality and law. But he does so by throwing on the carpet – and having them pass as cogent – neo-Enlightenment value judgements far from taken for granted: Habermas's argumentation, as I said, just makes a show of assuming 'metacritically' as an object of critical discussion positions of value pertaining to non-communicating systems of thought with his eternal Kantianism, and therefore not accepted in their inherent radicalism, which the ethics of discourse – this time not very ethically – prefers to ignore, if not entirely dispel.[13]

3. *Misrepresentations of Kant's universalism.* – To the first premise («the politics of human rights serve the purpose of imposing norms that are part of a universalist morality»), stated laconically and with a rather laboured «falsity»,[14] Habermas merely repeats himself by adding – in the initial phase – a series of plain historical facts:

Human rights in the modern sense dates back to the Virginia *Bill of Rights*, the American Declaration of Independence of 1776, and the Declaration of the Rights of Man and of the Citizen of 1789. These declarations were inspired by the political philosophy of rational-legal authority, particularly in Locke and Rousseau (ibid.).

These historical facts are intended to introduce, by presenting it rhetorically as non-problematic precisely because historically justified in such a way as to be postulated as definitive, the notion – actually very much debatable in a cultural context that is claimed to be fully secularised – of «superpositive validity» («*überpositive Geltung*»).[15] It should be noted in this regard that Habermas, usually so careful in his elaboration and in the use of his principles of interpretation, bends over backwards in order to avoid seeing the puritan theological-political substratum which is part and parcel of the concept of «inherent right» – the notion conceptually intrinsic to that of human rights and, I would add, in all value positions related to the idea of a universal morality.

In his proposed reconstruction, Habermas insists on the legality *ab origine* of fundamental rights (and human rights), in order to keep his theoretical position safe from the risks arising from an accusation of undue 'moralisation' of the political dimension, of which he is well aware and whose degree he is unwilling – in this case with undeniable intellectual honesty – to preventively underestimate.[16] But this recognition is not accompanied – as would be expected – by any serious inclination to doubt his value presuppositions, whose postulatory character is obvious.

Habermas's text needs to be studied very carefully. To Schmitt's remark, aimed at exposing the hypocritical moralising function of human rights, Habermas never tires repeating that:

the concept of 'human rights' does not have a moral origin, but is rather a specific form of the modern concept of 'individual rights', namely a specifically juridical category. Human rights have been *from the start* ['von Haus aus'] of a juridical nature. What gives them the appearance of moral rights is not their content [. . .], but rather a sense of validity [*Geltungssinn*] that projects them 'beyond' all national juridical systems.[17]

In other words: the fundamental rights (and with them the rights of man, which should form the foundation of the cosmopolitical community) are able to add a universal *moral content* (deriving from that trans-systemic «sense of validity» assumed unproblematically as common to all evolved juridical systems) with a *juridical structure* which makes them coercible (deriving in turn from the evolution of subjective rights positivised within the jurisdiction of the democratic *Rechtsstaat*). Which, if accepted, would make it possible to speak – with true short-circuit logic – of «universal rights» in the sense of being universally receivable, justified definitively in terms of rational argumentation. Habermas does not seem to entertain any doubts. It is true – he concedes – that «despite their *claim* to universal validity, human rights have been able to take on an unequivocally positive form only in the national juridical systems of democratic States», but it is also true that «they are waiting to be institutionalised within the framework of the cosmopolitical system which is coming to light in these years» [Habermas (1996): 25], where it is clear that this institutionalisation should by now resemble a sort of imperative. This is so since «the moral universalism that guided Kant's endeavor remains the fundamental intuition capable of establishing the guiding criteria [of a] practical-moral self-comprehension of modernity».[18]

It is disconcerting how Habermas can so nonchalantly put together, and pass as based on the level of argument, a series of statements (and correlative value judgements) of an ideological nature – and still anything but universal – of which he strives to hide the fact that it functions to serve a logic of interests whose success is certainly not due to the intrinsic goodness of the arguments that support it, but rather to a globally favourable balance of forces. What emerges here is the *strategic* nature of the Habermas project, vainly dissembled in exoteric forms dictated by the theory of communicative action: all in all – we can say – inspired by something not very different from the ancient intent of philosophers to justify that «might is right».

Habermas's strategy of argumentation proceeds in the direction of preventively denying the possibility of overall positions of alternative value, capable of establishing the democratic legitimacy of political identities not attributable to the project of organising a worldwide command centre. The generalising and neutralising rhetorical statements that accompany this design do nothing to mitigate the arrogant assumption that determines it: political identities non-compliant with the prevailing ideology (generally inspired by the rhetoric of human rights as the core of legitimacy of the domination exercised by the governing classes) *cannot* exist even in principle, because dangerous or regressive, for he takes for granted the goodness of a world order conceived self-praisingly as the extreme, epoch-making outcome of the historical and cultural Enlightenment project. In other words, no one (no individual, no people, no political community) would, in Habermas's intention, dare to question the desirability of a movement towards world unification and, as inevitable consequence, of a sacrifice of conflicting single wills, whatever shape or form – cultural, sociological, religious – they might take. These single wills must, as a foregone conclusion, be deemed backward, and possibly fall under the trite mechanisms of a line of reasoning that has as its prototype the *reductio ad Hitlerum*. (The ideological arrogance demonstrated by the governments of the European Union about the so-called «Haider case», in January 2000, takes on here a symbolic value.)

Let us consider these arguments which Habermas uses in his essay on the idea of Kant's 'perpetual peace' to convince himself that he is neutralising the critical potential of Schmitt's 'school of suspicion', evading – after a mock debate – its radical impact by reducing it to instances of a vulgar warmongering:

> Schmitt loads the concept of 'Political' with vitalistic valences because he wants to shore up his basic thesis: the creative force of the 'political' must necessarily revert to a destructive force as soon as it strays from the international arena of wolves in which it can release its 'conquering violence'. By promoting world peace, the global extension of human rights and democracy would – unintentionally – have the effect of destroying the limits characterising juridically compliant [*formgerecht*] war, authorised by the law of nations. Without this venting in free nature [*freie Wildbahn*], war would end up flooding the autonomous, civil spheres of life of modern societies, therefore annihilating all the complexity of differentiated societies. Actually, this admonition concerning the catastrophic consequences resulting from the obsolescence of war in terms of juridical pacifism refers to a metaphysic typical of an era, or rather of an aesthetic – today rather outmoded – of so-called 'storms of steel'.[19]

But Schmitt does not mean this. His intention is to describe and explain real phenomena which are integral to the dimension of the 'Political' – a distinct set of problems already as such qualitatively irregular with respect to the solely moralistic problems of humanity as *single moral subject*. The key point is rather that the general equality among human beings, axiomatic to the goal of humanity as a single moral subject (and therefore to the *effectiveness* of universal human rights) is not the goal of real politics, but – in a best-case scenario (one which does not simply provide an ideological cover for power plays) – a moral ideal of reference.

Kant himself would talk of «regulative idea» – an idea

that can never be ipso facto the subject of a juridical question, but that can become – and in fact often does – the most appropriate ideological weapon for prevailing in a political conflict. Who could resist a force that fights under the mantle of the universal value of humanity? And what 'inhuman' (as such easily criminalisable) subject could ultimately act as a counterforce for resisting as such the full realisation of the 'good of humanity'? It is in thinking alarmingly of this hypothesis of ideological discrimination from humanitarian motives that Schmitt argues that a moral ideal like that of 'humanity' does *not* in itself constitute a juridical question.[20]

The theoretical reasons for Schmitt's position appear already quite clear in texts of the late 1920s, thus much earlier than the years of *Ex captivitate salus* and *Glossarium*, and they acquire significant premonitory value in relation to our present-day universal ecumenism.

> The idea of human equality contains neither a juridical nor a political nor an economic criterion. Its importance for constitutional doctrine is that it pertains to liberal individualism and upholds the principle of fundamental rights. [. . .] The reference to this general human condition may mitigate certain harshnesses and act in a moderating and relativising direction, but it cannot constitute a concept [. . .]. An equality that has no other content than an equality as such common to all human beings would simply be a non-political equality since *it lacks the correlative concept of a possible inequality.* Every equality acquires its importance and its meaning on the basis of its correlation with a possible inequality. It is all the more intense the greater is the inequality in relation to those who are not part of the equals.[21]

It is certainly not by imputing to Schmitt's theory of the 'political' inevitable imperialist or warmongering consequences (and therefore blaming it for a kind of duality in prescriptive terms of the phenomena and regularities described) that Habermas can claim to exorcise the heuristically fruitful function exercised by this theory. But it is obvious that the real reason why Habermas needs to preventively discredit Schmitt's view is that he risks incurring its disruptive impact, condensed in its two constituent polemical statements, which – by specifying more clearly what has already been said (see above, note 10) – can be summarised as follows: *a*) it is precisely the politics of human rights that provokes wars which – masquerading as simple 'police actions' – take on a dangerous moral valence (dangerous primarily because 'absolutist'); *b*) this moralisation necessarily produces criminalisation: by branding one's adversary as an 'absolute enemy' of humanitarian truth and good, one justifies the most ruthless repression in favour of the 'humanitarian' re-establishment of that truth and good (hence the totalising logic of 'humanitarian wars').

4. *Three counter-theses on the rights of man.* – There is then, as is evident, an absolute logical incompatibility between the communicative-humanitarian *Gestalt* and the political-realist one, and one of the most significant aspects in which this incompatibility reveals itself lies in the ambiguous moralisation of law established by the rights of man (due ultimately to the confusion resulting from an instrumental reading of Kant's texts, between the two classic profiles – the moral one and the juridical one – of *Sollen*).[22] Here it is impossible not to note how there creeps into Habermas's text a serious contradiction between calling, on the one hand, *moral* the content of fundamental rights and *legal* the structure that determines its enforceability, and recognising, on the other, that the «sense of [universal moral] validity» (*Geltungssinn*) inherent in these 'rights' is only a *requirement*, or rather a «claim» (*Geltungsanspruch*) whose effectiveness is not (and cannot be) given, but only postulated on the basis of a need for justification which is not necessarily liable to be satisfied.

A need, therefore, and not an ascertained moral content; a claim, and not a reality, are the characteristics that determine the logical structure of the *Menschenrechte* in which Habermas tends to see fulfilled the prodigy (which one would not hesitate to define as theological, or rather, theological-political) of the encounter between ontology and morality, between being and having to be.

If we bear in mind this character of a «claim of validity» (*Geltungsanspruch*) as the constitutive element of the logical form of fundamental rights, then it is incorrect to state, as Habermas does, that

the fundamental rights governing such general subjects as moral arguments *are certainly sufficient to their foundation*. These are arguments that justify in what sense the assurance of these rules mirrors the interest of *all* [sic, E. C.] people as people, therefore in what sense these rules are good for *all*[23]

or even that

this universal validity, in relation to people as such, is a property that fundamental rights share with moral norms.[24]

These are rhetorical statements which are certainly unimpressive for their rational cogency, but which are justifiable in concrete terms only by postulating the existence of a political power able to enforce them, i.e. to be the sociological condition of their effectiveness. However, such statements betray their nature of dogmas of a claimed neo-Enlightenment political theology – unacknowledged on account of its very neo-Enlightenment claim – in their overlooking the fact, indubitable (and clear in the light of a realistic approach, which in this case too breaks down through a radical nominalistic analysis the eternal humanitaristic universalisms), for which:

1) the rights of man are conceptually a hybrid, located halfway between the juridical and the moral dimension.

A hybrid that holds up at the price of taking as a universal foundation of validity what is merely a justifying shell (Pareto would speak of mere «derivation») of the factual force that takes on the task of administering those very rights of man;

2) no juridical norm that has incorporated certain moral contents (even if it claims to raise them to the abstraction of «fundamental rights») can be universal. Only that which is purely formal, strictly speaking, universal, and this is certainly not the case for the rights of man;

3) no moral norm that aspires to universality can be applied on a practical level unless it is supported by a political force capable of imposing it. But then it can no longer be considered universal, but rather as a projection of this political force. (It is worth mentioning yet again that, as such, a moral norm can at best express a «request» for universality, but a request still originating from a partial subject, tied to concrete perspectives of interest, and not by any idealistic *dominus* of universality, to be viewed as the theological-political projection of the cumbersome Judeo-Christian God, even if in renewed forms of Kantian puritanism.)

These three theses, which impede the preachability of the rights of man as universal rights (and which we could for the sake of convenience call: 1) the thesis of the «justifying shell of interest»; 2) the thesis of «embedded moral content»; 3) the thesis of the «necessary ineffectiveness of universality») point out some very embarrassing truths for the new juris-globalist conformism, which sees in the politics of human rights – possibly framed in coercive terms – the virtuous realisation of an 'inescapable obligation of morality'. Who would dare – we asked ourselves earlier, ironically – take sides with 'evil' against 'good'? Habermas's relentless struggle against barely relativistic or 'contextualising' value positions[25] leads him to paradoxical (and just till yesterday embarrassing, at least for the left) appeals for an entirely German 'philosophical imperialism', vainly masked by a pan-communicative ideology, of which his essay on 'legitimation by way of human rights' offers significant examples.

In so doing, Habermas refers explicitly to Rawls' idea of so-called *overlapping consensus*,[26] according to which humanity should be put in a position finally to establish a peaceful coexistence, recognising in the medium of law – essentially in the form of human rights – the sole source of legitimation, valid for all civilisations (and not just for the Western one):

> Just as what happened to Christianity during the European religious schism, so too the traditional images of the world are being transformed today – under the impulse of the reflection induced by the modern conditions of life – into the 'reasonable comprehensive doctrines' of which Rawls speaks. By this he means an *ethical self-comprehension of the world and of the self* which – having become *reflective* – leaves the way open to *reasonably foreseeable disagreements with other religious beliefs*, with which it is nevertheless possible to agree on the rules of a juridically equalised coexistence.[27]

But it should be noted that all the key points of this quote are highly questionable. It is unclear how this supposed «reflectivity» is capable of bringing about the no less desired «ethical self-comprehension of the world and of the self»: we rather get the impression that his words have, in these contexts of philosophical analysis, miraculous effects, to the point that it should not be surprising to see the reflective method succeed in the difficult task of settling *radical value disagreements*, comparable to those that occur «with other religious beliefs».

This quasi-thaumaturgic virtue becomes highly implausible if ascribed to procedural reason. Through its effective «reflective» intervention it would be able to rationalise what is irrational, make negotiable what is non-negotiable, as well – at least in part – as juridicising the 'Political' by a recognition in it of conflicts which however are «reasonably foreseeable» and hence to our great relief relegated to the jurisdiction of the universal! It seems that Habermas, in voicing in passages such as this the needs of the Western political class (linked to social techno-bureaucracies, virtually or actually orphans of the welfare state and anxious to replace it with something equally profitable), has abandoned all 'philosophical' decorum, to the point of declaring indisputable what are just *some* of the possible options of ordinary political ideology. It is quite clear at this point why any 'hypernormative', moralistic politics wants at all costs to steer clear of direct confrontation with theoretical positions capable of unmasking its unilaterality.

We see here also the profound intellectual reasons for the incompatibility which exists between any normative political philosophy and Schmitt's theory of the 'Political' – an incompatibility whose clearly visible traces are present in Habermas's recent writings, taking the form of polemical outbursts which, far from being intellectually exhaustive, degenerate to the logic of political struggle. However, it is the *Streit um die Menschenrechte* which remains the principal form in which this larger conflict is presented, whose dimensions can well be defined as momentous, between a classical tradition of European thought and a new approach to what Pareto would call socialist morality, unknown – at least in the same form – before the mid twentieth century, and vigorously revived in the nineties after the fall of the Soviet empire.[28]

This ideological approach is ensconced by Habermas within his theory in the same terms in which it is launched on a planetary scale by the arrogant theology of humanity, whose roots can be found – as has often been noted – in the re-elaboration of the principal monotheistic religions in the forefront at the start of the third millennium.[29] The dual form in which this theology of humanity is presented – Judeo-Christian ecumenism – makes reference to a solidaristic, egalitarian moralism endowed with immense extortionist powers via the inculcation of guilt, against which Nietzsche's classic pages from the *Genealogy of Morals* remain more than ever timely. These values and thought systems today inspire and deeply determine the ideological orientations and the overall politics of the great pro-universalist powers such as the United States, caricatured by the European Union despite the profuse efforts at re-elaboration by opinion-makers such as Habermas.

5. *Conclusions.* – To sum up, I find completely unfounded the general thesis underpinning Habermas's argumentational system, namely that human rights do not belong to the category of *moral rights* (which we should translate, as has been said, simply as moral «claims»), but – from the start – to that of actual *legal rights*, in the form of «subjective rights», endowed with a specific enforceability which is recognised as the differential element determining its juridical stature. In particular, the theoretical solution proposed by Habermas concerning the problem of the relationship between the moral dimension and the legal dimension of human rights[30] appears unsatisfactory first of all on a logical basis. As we noted at the beginning of the previous paragraph, in Habermas's view «the juridical nature of the norms regards their structure, and not their content», which instead is moral and universal. Like other individual rights, human rights certainly have a moral content, but – apart from that moral content – they belong on the basis of their structure to a system of positive – and binding – law capable of establishing enforceable individual legal claims. For the moral establishment of human rights it would in other words be sufficient to believe that they regulate «such general matters» as to reflect «the interest of all persons qua persons».[31] Once again it should be stressed that this is a very weak, unrealistic theoretical solution: there can be no logical universal basis of argumentation for norms that are (as are necessarily juridical norms) related to particular positive-historical conditions. Which means that these requirements – universality and historicity, juridical

validity and moral absoluteness – cannot be simultaneously satisfied. As we have said, Habermas mistakes the claim to universal validity advanced for a certain class of norms – the *moral* norms related to human rights – for an already established claim to universal validity (and therefore effectiveness) of corresponding *juridical-positive* norms. The leap is abrupt and not formalisable in rigorous analytical terms. Perhaps only substantialist and intuitionistic premises typical of classical natural law, with their undemonstrable faith in a moral sense seen as infallible organ of judgement – secularisation of the Aristotelian-Thomist concept of *synderesis* – could explain, but not authorise, this self-sacralising mechanism of law: but explaining it on an openly metaphysical level, repudiated as such by those who, like Habermas, admit only procedural, public, verifiable conceptions of approach to value.

Of little worth, at this point, is the caution with which Habermas accompanies the delicate question of the 'immediate' implementation of moral value, considered in the form of humanitarian politics, which supports the judicial enforcement of the rights of man. The «kernel of truth» present in the realistic critique guided by the theory of the 'Political' towards such a 'judicial implementation' – Habermas admits – is that «an *immediate* moralisation of law and politics would actually break down those "protected areas" that we [. . .] still want to safeguard», so that «it would produce in the international arena [. . .] harmful effects».[32] But – Habermas continues – the risk is only apparent, and the damaging effects of 'moral fundamentalism' can be easily averted. In fact:

> the politics of human rights carried forward by a world organisation revert to a fundamentalism of human rights [*Menschenrechtsfundamentalismus*] only when they provide moral legitimation, under the cloak of a juridical pseudo-legitimation, to an armed intervention which in fact merely expresses the struggle of one party against another. In cases such as these the world

organisation (or the alliance acting on its behalf) would commit a 'deception', presenting as a police measure – neutral and justified by executory laws and judgements – what in truth would simply be a military confrontation between warring factions.[33]

The point is that, in the light of what any serious, realistic investigation shows, this is what *always and necessarily* occurs: knowledge of the laws inherent in the logic of value,[34] on the one hand, and the realist unmasking of rhetorical weapons, which universalist morality uses on the other, no longer permit any illusions about the fact that Habermas's thesis of the pristine, indestructible juridical stature of the rights of man (seen as an evolutive form in the framework of the cosmopolis, of the subjective rights of the classic liberal State)[35] is an ideological thesis endowed with a precise function of post-natural-law legitimation of the power structures functional to the domain of certain political parties, which obviously cannot pretend to be a 'totality', but which are aware that only this fiction makes the exercise of their command admissible.

The matter is all the more serious if one thinks that Habermas has hinging on the results of this false demonstration the approach to, and then solution of, the fundamental problem thrown on the carpet by political realism, leading back to the charge by which «a policy of intervention on human rights must necessarily degenerate into a "fight against evil"» (Habermas 1996: 206) and «total war is simply the form taken by that "just war" in which any intervention policy in favor of human rights necessarily culminates» (ibid. p. 209). The inevitable consequence is then – and, we have said, could not be otherwise – to immediately criminalise one's opponent by striking him harder thanks to the monopoly of moral justification retained by the culturally (and militarily) prevailing 'humanitarian' coalition forces. Military actions – renamed and hence legitimated as «police actions» – would then aim at restoring a moral order of the world treacherously dashed by the political criminal of the moment, while the neutrality of cosmopolitical jurisdiction would function as a universal steriliser, with the specific purpose of extirpating the dimension of the 'political' embodied by any form of political existence that is 'particular', resistant – precisely because of this peculiarity – to standardisation.

There are those who, like the sociologist Belohradsky, have recently reactivated in this very perspective the realist critique of the instrumental use of the idea of «neutrality», by observing how modern politics are entirely focused on the desire to «neutralise», that is to say to proceed towards a continual dislocation of potential places of conflict, to the quest – by its very nature endless – for a claim to rationality able to regulate by law all conflicts. It is clear that by going down this road one overlooks the fact that the terrain on which the political form of human existence rests can never be made neutral, or – what amounts to the same thing – pacified in the sublimated form of universality, under the jurisdiction of a procedural reason understood as the supreme protection and bulwark of impartiality.[36] Here, it must be said, impartiality is mystification. And it is significant to have to point out in relation to the thesis of an author like Habermas, who was born as a 'culture critic', in spite of his transition from a radical critique of society to a sophisticated (and devitalised) form of Kantianism. Certainly, such 'twists and turns' would have been considered just a few decades ago with far greater suspicion by European thought, then perhaps – it must be said – more demanding than today.[37]

We must, in the end, have the courage to recognise that human rights – far from being a momentous, definitive acquisition – are a simple ideology that expresses the eternal struggle to exercise a momentary tyranny, justified in moral terms, over the general system of values,[38] and as such are closely linked to a specific historical-cultural context (that produced by the global dominance of American power politics), which provides their sociological condition of possibility.

This ideology is based on the rejection of the categories of the 'political' and in particular of the workability of the friend/enemy distinction, which – by a kind of irony – returns periodically to emerge even in violent forms, even though (or, we should believe, just because) unexplained. Moralisation prevents it from being intelligible, because the neutralising concept of humanity by definition excludes that of enemy.[39] This makes it clear for what real purposes the idea of crimes against humanity, on the basis of which the international human rights police claims legitimacy, can only result in what one might call a true *principle of political management of the moral discrimination* of forms of life extraneous to the prevailing project of the socialist fulfilment of modernity, therefore as opponents. It should be recognised that law, in the form of the universalist administration of the rights of man, is hence degraded – contrarily to what Habermas himself would like – to a questionable tool of moral propaganda, exposing the connection between propaganda and humanity which Gottfried Benn, with extraordinary premonition, had long derided.[40]

Notes

Chapter I

1. Of course, this 'representability' should – in turn – be immediately problematised. We should recall that Western metaphysics, at least in its major currents (among them Thomistic *philosophia perennis*, as well as secular metaphysical idealism), is based wholly on the presupposition (i.e. fiction) of absolute transparency in the representation of entities. We could say that it is all representative instinct: an instinct that subordinates – and sacrifices – the problem of truth to the needs of systems and of speakability.

2. The «grande visione d'insieme»: so Lombardi Vallauri 1999: 7–112, in the introduction to the research he coordinated on *Logos dell'Essere – Logos della norma*, entitled *Dio o Logos? La grande visione d'insieme alla prova*.

3. And this, as Leibniz expressly states in his *Monadology* (I, 43), since «God's intellect is the seat of eternal truths or of the ideas on which they depend». The very principles of natural law reside in the divine intellect: «alia ergo sublimiora et meliora iuris principia quaerenda sunt, non tantum in voluntate divina, sed in intellectu, nec tantum in potentia Dei, sed in sapientia» (G. W. Leibniz, *Opera*, Ed. Dutens, IV, 3, p. 272). See on this point Jalabert 1960.

4. But, in truth, only this possibility, which is not given, to «go beyond» would enable us to talk about the universality of logos as a valid transcendental structure «in all possible worlds».

5. However, even 'pure' conventionalism encounters serious problems: I limit myself to referring on this point to the observations of Amsterdamski 1978. See, in the first corollary of this volume, a discussion of the modern origins of conventionalism in the ethical-political and epistemological sphere.

6. On Schmitt's arguments in *Politische Theologie I e II* see further ahead in Corollary II. See also, concerning Blumenberg's interpretation of *Politische Theologie II*, W. Hübener, *Carl Schmitt und Hans Blumenberg oder über Kette und Schuss in der historischen Textur der Moderne*, in J. Taubes 1983, Bd. I: *Der Fürst dieser Welt*. More generally, see the whole first section of the volume edited by Taubes, with contributions, among others, by Böckenförde, Lübbe, Marquard and Koslowski. We recall how Schmitt tended to favour, among the various possible meanings of the concept of political theology, precisely that of a «structural analogy» between theological concepts and juridical ones, determined by a «systematische Strukturverwandtschaft» of theology and jurisprudence. (On this point see also Chapter IV.)

7. Thus Lombardi Vallauri 1999: 11–16.

Chapter II

1. Lombardi Vallauri 1999, ibid.

2. Spinoza, *TTP*: 377–9, italics mine.

3. So A. Droetto (1980: 396, note 17). He writes: «This eternal order, namely the *lex divina* of Chapter IV, which links more closely the *Tractatus* to the doctrine of the *Ethics* and the *De intellectus emendatione*, is Spinoza's true concept of natural law: his true 'guide to reason', whereby human beings, rather than being averse, 'always necessarily agree' (and not by their own consent) with persons who, in turn, live in their own way according to nature». See Spinoza, *Eth.*, IV, prop. XXIV e XXXV; Spinoza, *TP*, II, 6.

4. See the more recent interesting essay by Biuso 1991: 93 ff.: «As a partial mode of one of the infinite attributes of

eternal substance, man is reconducted by Spinoza to his immediate reality as a particle, alternatingly harmonious and rebellious, of a metaphysical universe that still goes on as it should, independently of human desire and fear. [. . .] God is not the name of a creator, officer, judge who is separate from entities in a place all his own. A dimension of sacrality unto itself and separate is not given. The divinity of the world and the total worldliness of the divine sanction the absolute blessing of being in its every small and great expression» (121).

5. Which also authorises sustaining, generically, that the very logical-analytical model of Western philosophical rationalism is constructed on a theological model, for the most part unwittingly assumed and not critically discussed.

6. *Met.*, V, 12, 1019a, 18–24, italics mine.

7. Ibid. 1019b, 1–4.

8. *Met.*, IX, 1, 1046a, 5–12. In *Met.*, V, 12, 1020a, 5 *dynamis* was already defined as *arché metabletiké en allo* («principle of change into something else»).

9. It is therefore true that «perhaps a substance has the potency to be and that, nonetheless, it does not exist, and – also – that a substance has the potency not to be and that, nonetheless, it exists» (*Met.*, IX, 3, 1047a, 20–21), although «he would not be telling the truth who, not taking into account that the impossible exists, would say that it is possible for the diagonal to be equal to a side, but that nonethless it will never be equal» (IX , 4, 1047b, 7–13), since what is logically contradictory is not inclined to exist, already at the stage of pure potency unrealised in action. «For this reason, if one willed or desired to do, at the same time, two different or contrary things, he could not do so; in fact he does not possess in this way the potency to do opposite things at the same time» (IX, 5, 1048, 21–3).

10. J. Beaufret, *Enérgeia et actus*, in id. 1973, vol. I: 123–4.

11. Ibid.

12. We recall that Cicero did not hesitate to the define the

concept of cause (Artistotle's *aitía*) as «id quod cuique . . . efficienter antecedit» (*De Fato*, XV).

13. Beaufret, *Enérgeia et actus*, in id. 1973: 125.

14. Thus Beaufret, ibid. p. 135: «It was as a result of a centuries-old toiling over the first words of *Genesis* that a metaphysical justification was at last granted. But at what price? The price of the "translation" of the Greek *enérgeia* with *actus*: a "translation" that absolutely does not carry the sense of a return to Aristotle – as Aquinas thought – but that, on the contrary, brings about a decisive distancing, although Aquinas might not have been aware of it. In this discrepancy, much more essential than the one formed by monotheism, lies the difference that diametrically contrasts Aquinas with Aristotle. We might formulate it in these terms: Aquinas, starting from the biblical narrative (which he had *visibly* before his eyes) and from the Latinisation of the Greek (which instead was invisible to him), brings the Latin *agere* and its *actus* into the very idea of being, since he believes that the most appropriate term for designating being is *actualitas*, whereas Aristotle meant to purify his representation of its cause of any reference to action. No more complete an overturning, under the guise of a claimed identity, can be imagined.»

15. Heidegger 1957: 136.

16. Beaufret, *Note sur Platon et Aristote*, in id. 1973: 112.

17. Gilson 1948: 61.

18. See Castrucci 1985, part IV.

19. See especially *Eth.*, I, Appendix: a really fundamental text for understanding Spinoza's final intentions regarding his philosophical proof.

20. Agamben 1993: 250, 245.

21. «1277 marked a victory for the concept of divine omnipotence, since many of the condemned articles restricted the freedom of God and affirmed the necessity of the world and the laws of nature.» In this sense Courtenay 1985: 252. See in particular on this topic Hissette 1977.

22. See Muckle 1933, with precise information on Al-Ghazali's

fundamental work *Tahafut* (1928, 1958). On the points we are discussing, see in particular W. J. Courtenay 1973: 77–94.

23. Agamben 1993: 248. As Gilson observes about the Muslim sect of the Ash'arites, «The metaphysical elaboration of these religious principles led [. . .] to a curious and original conception of the universe. Everything there was disjointed in time and space to make it possible for God's omnipotence to circulate easily. A substance composed of disjointed atoms, that lasts for a period of time composed of disjointed moments, *which performs operations in which every moment is independent of the preceding one and with no effect on what follows, the whole non-subsistent, held together and functioning only by God's will, which keeps it above nothingness and animates it with its effectiveness, this was pretty much the world of the Ash'arites.* It strongly influenced Maimonides and, after him, Aquinas. It was a combination of *atomism* and *occasionalism* caused by a religious jealousy of divine omnipotence» (Gilson 1952: 348–9, italics mine).

24. In the same sense in which Blondel spoke of an «anticartesianism» of Malebranche, that is of a philosophy visibly freed from Cartesian rationalism: Blondel 1916, on which see Del Noce 1965: 596.

25. Al-Ghazali, *Tahafut*. See G. Agamben 1993: 248.

26. Agamben 1993: 248–9, italics mine.

27. Agamben 1993: 253.

28. Welzel 1962.

29. Welzel 1962 quotes Duns Scotus, *Ox.*, I, dist. 35, *qu. unica*, n. 12: «Idea est ratio aeterna in mente divina, secundum quam aliquid est formabile extra secundum propriam rationem eius» (see Welzel, p. 73, n. 46). Already for St Augustine (*De diversis quaestionibus*, LXXXIII, qu. 46 «De ideis») ideas are platonically initial forms or concepts of things, eternal, immutable and always equal to themselves. God – Welzel notes – «formed the world according to these ideas. They are the laws of the divine government of the world, in them all that is unstable follows

its temporal course under an infallible guide. *Augustine places in God's mind the ideas that for Plato remained in a hyperuranial dimension.* [. . .] When God created things he did not look at models placed outside of his spirit: to say this would be blasphemous. Instead all the mental models according to which things may have been or have been created are *contents of the mind of God*, and because everything that is in the mind of God is eternal and immutable, ideas are true, eternal and immutable» (ibid. pp. 76–7). Welzel concludes that «In these words of Augustine's it is remarkable that he not only considered ideas as *thoughts of God*, but founded their eternity and immutability precisely on their belonging in the mind of God, and not in and of themselves. God's knowledge, Augustine says somewhere else (*De Trinitate*, XV, 13) does not depend on the existence of things, but the existence of things depends on God's knowledge –: a thought that recalls the doctrine of Duns Scotus *of God's productive intelligence*, and that *inserts into the Platonic doctrine of ideas a "voluntaristic" aspect alien to it*» (ibid., italics mine).

30. Aquinas, *Summa Theologica*, I, qu. 15 ad 3.
31. Welzel 1962: 74: «Diese etwas "mystische" Lehre des Duns Scotus von der produktiven Intelligenz Gottes [. . .] ist offenbar durch das Bestreben diktiert, die Ideen, deren Existenz Duns nicht leugnen konnte, doch von Gottes Wesenheit abzusetzen und ihr unterzuordnen.»
32. *Ox.*, I, dist. 44, *qu. unica*, n. 2, to which we will return.
33. This clear primacy of divine will (Welzel again notes) harks back to Plato's position as expressed in his *Euthyphro*, which Duns Scotus paraphrased in several points of his work, including *Ox.*, III, dist. 19, qu. 1, n. 7: «omne aliud a Deo ideo est bonum quia a Deo volitum, et non converso . . . quia est bonum ideo acceptum». But as Welzel goes on to say, in this emphatic insistence on God's will, 'who assures us that God does not will our loss?' In this sense Welzel 1962: 74–5. In other words, why should God necessarily be considered as absolute *bonitas*, indeed as unique *bonum* in itself? The human

species could, in fact, not be guaranteed this *amor Dei*. (This was a theme of Gnostic origin that Bayle later developed and that Giuseppe Rensi would return to more than once in the early decades of this century.) Welzel, however, sees in this «doctrine of the essential goodness» of God «an idealistic residue of metaphysics, in particular voluntaristic, of Duns Scotus» (ibid. p. 75).

34. Welzel 1962: 77. Gilson 1952 is, if possible, even clearer on this point: «[Duns Scotus and Ockham] both want to avoid the same danger. They have constantly before them the thought of Averroes' God as pure Intellect, or Avicenna's God, whose will necessarily follows the law of his intellect. The God they appeal to is Jehovah, *who obeys nothing, not even ideas. In order to free him from this necessity, Duns Scotus subordinated them to God as much as he could without considering them as creations; Ockham solves the problem differently, by suppressing them.* Here he goes far beyond Abelard, who considered ideas as the privilege of divine knowledge. Ockham suppresses the reality of universals even in God. It is also because there are no ideas in God that there is no universal in things. Why should there be? *What we call ideas is nothing but the very things that God can produce: ipsae ideae sunt ipsaemet res in Deo producibiles*» (653, italics mine). And Paul Vignaux: «Ockham still speaks of ideas, but the historian needs to explain that for him, *since God is radically simple, there are no divine ideas*; his essence therefore is neither the origin of ideas, as for Duns Scotus, nor the place of ideas, as for Aquinas: here there appears, so to speak, the personality of the Ockhamist God, face-to-face with the Thomist or the Scotist God, but also the Cartesian God, radically simple, but essentially active: *causa sui*.» Quoted from Gilson 1952, ibid., italics mine.

Chapter III

1. Agamben (1993), p. 254.
2. Aquinas, *Summa Theologica*, I, qu. 19, art. 1: «Voluntas

enim intellectum consequitur». It has been commented: «By attributing efficient causality to God, Aquinas is compelled to preserve or restore the distinction between God's intellect and God's will. [This] distinction is to be regarded as a distinction of reason and not in any way a real distinction». Thus E. L. Fortin, in L. Strauss and J. Cropsey, eds (1987): 269.

3. *Summa Theologica*, I, qu. 19, art. 2, italics mine.
4. «The intellect guides the will, the will for its part commands potency, which executes. But [. . .] the whole movement of the intellect lies in the will» (*Quaestiones disputatae*, I, art. 5, resp.).
5. *Quaestiones disputatae*, I, art. 3.
6. St Augustine, *De Civitate Dei*, X, 31.
7. *Quaestiones disputatae*, III, art. 14.
8. Already Hugh of Saint Victor, writing in the twelfth century, offered this detailed account of divine omnipotence: «Deus ergo summe potens est, [. . .] nec ideo minus potest quia impossibile non potest; "impossibilia posse" non est posse, sed non posse» (Hugh of St Victor, *De sacramentis christianae fidei*, in Migne, *Patr. Lat.*, CLXXVI, c. 216).
9. *Quaestiones disputatae*, I, art. 7, italics mine.
10. Among the works sensitive to this problematic aspect, I limit myself to referring, with no claim to completeness, to Oakley 1961, 1968, 1984; Marrone 1974; Stratenwerth 1951; Miethke 1969; Pernoud 1970, 1972; Bannach 1975; Courtenay 1984.
11. Petrus de Tarantasia, *Sent.*, I, dist. 43, qu. 2, a. 4.
12. Randi 1986a, Chapter II.
13. «Dicunt iuristae quod quis potest hoc facere *de facto*, hoc est de potentia sua absoluta, vel *de iure*, hoc est de potentia ordinata secundum iura» (*Ox.*, I, dist. 44, *qu. unica*, n. 1).
14. «In omni agente per intellectum et voluntatem, *potentem* conformiter agere legi rectae et tamen *non necessario* conformiter agere legi rectae, est distinguere potentiam *ordinatam* a potentia *absoluta*; et ratio huius est, quia

potest agere conformiter illi legi rectae, et tunc secundum potentiam ordinatam (ordinata enim est in quantum est principium exequendi aliqua conformiter legi rectae secundum *ordinem* praefixum ab illa lege), et potest agere praeter illam legem vel contra eam, et in hoc est potentia absoluta, excedens potentiam ordinatam» (Duns Scotus, *Ox.*, I, dist. 44, *qu. unica*, n. 1). See recently on this point Schütz 2012.

15. «Quando *in potestate agentis* est lex et rectitudo eius, ita quod non est recta nisi quia est ab illo statuta, tunc potest *recte* agere agendo aliter quam lex illa dictet, quia tunc potest statuere aliam legem rectam, secundum quam agat ordinate; nec tunc potentia sua absoluta simpliciter excedit potentiam ordinatam, quia tunc esset ordinata secundum illam aliam legem» (ibid. n. 1).

16. Randi 1986a, p. 72.

17. «Ideo sicut [Deus] potest aliter agere ita potest aliam legem statuere rectam; quae si statueretur a Deo, recta esset, quia nulla lex est recta nisi quatenus a voluntate divina acceptante statuta. [. . .] Non quidem fieret ordinate secundum istum ordinem, sed fieret ordinate secundum alium ordinem; quem alium ordinem ita posset voluntas divina statuere, sicut aliter potest agere» (*Ox.*, I, dist. 44, *qu. unica*, n. 2).

18. Courtenay 1985: 253–4, comments: «God could have acted and still could act otherwise (*potest aliter agere*). But Scotus acknowledged that any other action could result in another order (and thus God can never act *inordinate*) not so much because of the consistency of the divine nature but because whatever system God institutes becomes right and just on the grounds that God has chosen it.» Also Randi (1986a), p. 65: «It is not difficult to see in this line the seeds of possible absolutist developments. Each system appears to be hanging by the will of him or them who with respect to it have the faculty of *dispensatio* [. . .], with a downward movement that – from God to man – is gradually restricted to the areas of availability.» This is not so much – we believe – a matter of detecting

possible 'absolutist' developments, so as to perceive in these thought patterns a constant of political theology, which goes far beyond the model of absolutism and denotes instead the entire logical and epistemological structure of 'modernity'. See on this point the interesting ideas contained in a brief article by Randi 1986b: 129–38. It is well known that some scholars have seen in the theology of Scotus (and Ockham) an important starting point for understanding the structure of modern political philosophy. So A. de Muralt 1978, esp. 10 ff. But previously Tierno Galván 1951, now in id. 1971. Notations of this type are encountered in Villey 1975, as well as in the work – of a very different nature – Blumenberg 1974, esp. during the whole of the second part of the volume, dedicated to the concept of «theologischer Absolutismus».

19. Gilson 1952: 654. On Ockham's concept of freedom see Clark 1978: 122–60.

20. For Clark it is true that «it is not the special dispensation or the miraculous intervention of God that troubles Ockham, but rather the possibility that God might have ordained (*potuit ordinasse*) an universe in which He alone would be a causal agent» (ibid. p. 127, n. 9). He adds precisely: «man's perception of the world would not be altered if occasionalism obtained» (ibid.).

21. Agamben 1993: 261–2 (also for the preceding quotation from Leibniz).

22. Ockham, *TcB*, in id., *Opera politica*, vol. III: 234: «Et ideo, licet potentia Dei sit una, tamen propter diversam locutionem dicitur quod *Deus aliqua potest de potentia absoluta quae tamen numquam faciet de potentia ordinata* (hoc est, *de facto numquam faciet*)» (italics mine).

23. Randi 1986a: 67.

24. Ockham, *Quodlibeta*, in id., *Opera philosophica et theologica*, vol. IX: 585–6. See on this point L. Baudry 1958, *sub voce* «Potentia absoluta»: 205.

25. Gregory 1982: 517–27. See also A. de Muralt 1966: 159–91.

26. Courtenay 1974: 51.

27. Vignaux 1931, *sub voce* «Nominalisme», in *Dictionnaire*

de Théologie Catholique, tome XI/1, col. 734, observes with regard to Ockham's anti-realist criticism that «tous ceux qu'il avait lus étaient, en ce point, ses adversaires». He adds (*sub voce* «Occam», ibid. col. 877): «Occam a compté pour ses adversaires les maîtres qu'il connaissait: le réalisme des universaux est une doctrine commune: "omnes quos vidi concordant, dicentes quod natura quae est aliquo modo universalis, saltem in potentia et incomplete, est realiter in individuo" (*Sent.*, I, dist. 2, qu. 7B)».

28. Villey 1975: 213, 216.

Chapter IV

1. See Blumenberg 1969 and 1974. See also, on the concept of secularisation, Löwith, in «Philosophische Rundschau», XVI (1968).

2. Strictly speaking, more than of analogy, Leibniz speaks of derivation of the (structure of) theology from the (structure of) universal jurisprudence, seeing in the latter a *genus* which includes law (in the strict sense) and theology: «Nec mirum est, quod in Jurisprudentia, idem et usu come in Theologia usu venire, *quia Theologia species quaedam east Jurisprudentiae universim sumtae*, agit enim de iure et legibus obtinentibus in republica aut potius regno Dei super homines» (Leibniz, *Nova methodus*, pars specialis, § 2, italics mine).

3. Schmitt 1922: 49: «All the most meaningful concepts of the modern doctrine of the State are secularised theological ones. Not only on the basis of their historical development, since they passed to the doctrine of the State from theology, such as almighty God who became the all-powerful legislator, but also in their systematic structure, knowledge of which is necessary for a sociological consideration of these concepts.»

4. Kelsen 1922–3: 261–84.

5. Ibid.

6. As Randi has observed, «for Ockham it is necessary to admit that God has the power to produce at once any

effect normally produced through secondary causes; that God preserves intact his omnipotence, which extends on both the past and the future; that God cannot be bound by his creation. These theological needs are met by the concept of *potentia absoluta*, whose function is limited to safeguarding the contingency of reality and the freedom of God without affecting the regularity or intelligibility of reality» (Randi 1986a: 75).

7. Atger 1906: 136. At least on this point Hobbes's model would seem comparable with Descartes'.

8. Muralt 1978: 34–5. «Il suffit donc en contexte occamien et nominaliste d'éliminer d'une manière ou d'une autre la notion de Dieu du champ de la spéculation philosophique, pour dégager celle de la liberté humaine dans son amplitude infinie» (p. 34).

9. «Ista nomina (furtum, adulterium, odium, etc.) significant tales actus non absolute, sed connotando vel dando intelligere, quod faciens tales actus per praeceptum divinum obligatur ad oppositum . . . Si autem caderet sub praecepto divino, tunc faciens tales actus non obligaretur ad oppositum et per consequens tunc non nominaretur furtum, adulterium, etc.» (Ockham, *Sent.*, II, qu. 19 O).

10. Welzel 1962: 83.

11. Ibid. p. 112.

12. Ibid. Still fundamental on this point are the two essays by Buddeberg 1936–7 and 1937.

13. Welzel 1962: 112.

14. Thus Lombardi Vallauri 1999. See above, Chapter I, note 2.

15. Welzel 1962: 84: «Für Ockham gibt es überhaupt kein essentiell gutes Gesetz mehr, sondern nur noch einen essentiell guten Gesetzgeber.»

16. Rousseau, *Le contrat social*, II, 7, italics mine.

17. Schmitt 1921; 1928^2: 108, note 1. See Riley 1986.

18. See on these points Grua 1953: 267 ff. («Les essences, objet de l'intelligence divine»).

19. Bayle, *Continuation des pensées diverses sur la comète*, vol. II, Chapter 152 (= Leibniz, *Theodicea*, § 183).

20. Ibid., italics mine.
21. *Theodicea*, § 335.
22. *Theodicea*, § 183.
23. Leibniz, as is known, having found nothing better to say on this point, resorted to begging the question, in the form of the dogma of his theodicy: God does not will evil, and it is not God who creates it. «God allowed evil because *it is part the best project that exists in the region of the possible*, the project that the supreme wisdom could not help but choose» (*Theod.*, § 335). See Grua 1953: 346 ff. (Part II, Chapter X: «Le mal»).
24. «Cum enim consistat justitia in congruitate ac propor-tionalitate quadam, potest intelligi justum aliquid esse, etsi nec si qui justitiam exerceat nec in quem exerceatur, prorsus ut numerorum rationes sunt verae, etsi non sit nec qui numeret nec quod numeretur . . .» (G. W. Leibniz, quoted from Mollat 1885: 24 ff.).
25. Welzel 1962: 143–4.
26. Ibid. p. 144.
27. «Special beings endowed with intelligence may have laws that they themselves made, but also those they did not make. Beings endowed with intelligence, before existing, were possible: therefore they had relationships, and therefore possible laws. *Before laws were made, there existed possible relationships of justice.* To say that only what positive laws prohibit or ordain is right or wrong, is tan-tamount to saying that not all radii were equal before the circle was traced» (Montesquieu, *Esprit des lois*, I, 1, italics mine). On these topics see now Gazzolo 2014.
28. Spinoza's line of reasoning goes, in this sense, from the proposition «God does not work in terms of free will» (*Eth.*, I, prop. 32, corollary 1) to the wide-ranging discus-sion in the *Appendix*, already mentioned several times, to book I: «All things have been predetermined by God, not by the freedom of his will, that is by his absolute approval, but by God's absolute nature, that is, by God's infinite potency [. . .] And since all the prejudices I indicate depend on this only, that, namely, people

commonly suppose that all natural things, like themselves, *act for a purpose*, and they assert as a certainty that God himself guides all things towards a certain end – in fact, they say that God made all things for mankind, and mankind so that it should adore him – thus I shall consider firstly this prejudice alone, seeking primarily the reason why most people take comfort in him, and all, by nature, are so inclined to embrace him. I shall prove its falsity, and lastly the way in which their prejudices concerning good and evil, merit and sin, praise and blame, order and confusion, beauty and deformity, and other such things, have arisen» (ibid., italics mine). See the exact observations of Landucci 1992: 23–51 (especially: 34 ff.).

29. On the Spinoza–Leibniz relationship, see Belaval 1983: 531–52.

30. *Eth.*, I, Appendix, cit.

31. *Eth.*, II, prop. 3, scholium, italics mine. Spinoza's polemic proceeds with keen determination on that vast field of the theological-political imagination, a detailed map of which is provided by works such as those of Figgis 1934 or Kantorowicz 1957, by now justly considered classics.

32. This is the main meaning that – as is known – Schmitt 1922: 58 ff., assigns to 'political theology', from his awareness that «the metaphysical framework that a given work constructs of the world has the same structure as what occurs at first sight as the form of its political organisation». On this point see also the definitions present in Corollary II.

33. This does not mean that the theoretical analysis elicits an absolutistically obligatory result, as if it were a necessary reprise of Meinecke's *Idee der Staatsräson*. The free productivity of human potency can also be interpreted, as Spinoza does, in a radically democratic sense, by polarising attention on the concept of *'multitudo'*, of individuals, which appears repeatedly in the *Tractatus Politicus*. Consider the centrality of the following passages: «This right, which is defined by the potency of the *multitude*,

may be called power» (Spinoza, *TP*, II, 17, italics mine). «The right of power, that is of the highest authority, is nothing but natural law itself, determined by the potency no longer of each individual, but of the multitude, guided as by a single mind; or, as each individual exists in the state of nature, *so that unity of mind and body that is collective power has as much right as its potency is able to exert*» (*TP*, III, 2, italics mine). An original interpretation of these passages is given by Negri 1982, especially 225 ff., and in addition, on the idea of constituent power, Negri 1992, both texts stretching Spinoza's original intentions towards a literally *collectivist* metaphysics.

34. *TP*, III, 7.
35. See in general McIlwain's 1940 and Corwin's 1928-9 classic works. Corwin, in particular, postulates the existence of a clear historiographic line of continuity signalling the immutable character attributed to 'supreme law', from the thought of Cicero and the Stoics, passing through John of Salisbury, Bracton, Fortescue, Coke, up to American constitutionalism. According to this line – Corwin argues 1928-9: 21 – «there are certain principles of law that cannot fail to establish themselves by their intrinsic excellence, regardless of the attitude of those who control the material resources of the community. *These principles are not of human origin*; in truth, though they do not precede the divinity itself, they nevertheless express its nature enough to bind it and determine its extent. They are above any will as such, and pervade any reason. *They are eternal and immutable.* Of these principles human laws, when they are such that they must be obeyed, except for those relating to inessential matters, are nothing more than a document or a transcription, so that their adoption is *an act of pure recognition and of a declaratory nature*, and not an act of will or a manifestation of power» (italics mine).
36. An interpretation that does not allow itself to be enclosed, in my opinion, in the excessively unilateral observations contained in the fifth chapter of Schmitt 1938, which in

truth is one of the few places where Schmitt intervenes *directly* on Spinoza.

37. From a somewhat different point of view, Negri is in agreement in this awareness 1992, especially 35, and in general in the whole of Chapter I: *Constituent power: the concept of a crisis*. Negri insists on the logical link between constituent power and substantive democracy: «Constitutionalism is claimed a theory and practice of limited government: limited by the judicial review of administrative acts and, above all, limited through the organisation of the constituent power of the law [. . .]. The constitutionalist paradigm is always that of a "mixed constitution", of mediation of and in inequality, therefore an undemocratic paradigm. By contrast, the paradigm of constituent power is a force that erupts, cracks, breaks, disrupts any existing equilibrium and any possible continuity. Constituent power is linked to the idea of democracy as absolute power» (ibid. pp. 17–18). See more recently, on the Spinoza–Schmitt relationship, Walther 1993: 361–71.

38. Schmitt 1921; 1928[2]: 142. The theoretical and legal literature on the concept of constituent power is very extensive, if not always illuminating. Since Zweig's historical and doctrinal reconstruction (1909), I recall, among the most important works on the legal concept of constituent power, only: Sauerwein 1960; Steiner 1966; Böckenförde 1986.

39. Schmitt 1921; 1928[2]: 142.

40. Schmitt 1928: 79–80.

41. See on this point Breuer 1984, whose critical observations are, however, not always reliable.

42. Just as Schmitt notoriously developed a «Hobbesian crystal» in his well-known integrative note to § 7 of the *Begriff des Politischen*. On this topic, and on the importance in relation to this topic of Karl-Heinz Ilting, see Becchi 1995. So Schmitt 1963a: 121–3:

Notes

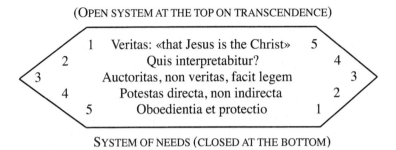

(OPEN SYSTEM AT THE TOP ON TRANSCENDENCE)

1	Veritas: «that Jesus is the Christ»	5	
2	Quis interpretabitur?		4
3	Auctoritas, non veritas, facit legem		3
4	Potestas directa, non indirecta		2
5	Oboedientia et protectio	1	

SYSTEM OF NEEDS (CLOSED AT THE BOTTOM)

The «Spinozan crystal» might take this form:

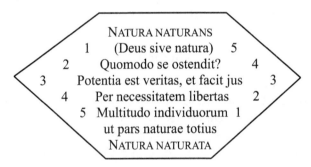

NATURA NATURANS
1 (Deus sive natura) 5
2 Quomodo se ostendit? 4
3 Potentia est veritas, et facit jus 3
4 Per necessitatem libertas 2
5 Multitudo individuorum 1
ut pars naturae totius
NATURA NATURATA

The Spinozan crystal is a closed ontological system, at both top and bottom. Between *natura naturans* and *natura naturata* there develops a continuous circuit, based on the «exposition», or rather the «expression», in the sense G. Deleuze 1978 gives to it, of only substance-*natura naturans* in the finite modes of *natura naturata*. The main question, homologous to Hobbes's *Quis interpretabitur?*, is *Quomodo (Deus sive natura naturans) se ostendit?*, to which the central axis responds 3 – 3 *Potentia est veritas, et facit jus*, which contemplates the reduction of truth to power: the 'contextuality' of truth and potency. No differently, (natural) right proceeds from (natural) potency. The *ratio* that inspires this process in immanence is the identity of freedom and necessity with regard to human

147

action. The ontological basis, then, on which the system rests is the material multitude of individuals as finite modes of the only infinite substance and as part of overall *natura naturata* (which includes the extra-human physical world). This means: the individual as modus *infinitae substantiae et particula naturae totius*. This involves, in the field of political theory, the concept of the State as democratic *respublica*, a single body composed of the sum of individual potencies and freedoms, «a potency no longer of each individual, but of the multitude, guided as one mind» (*TP*, III, 2). But, obviously, these points can only be mentioned here in passing.

43. See also Corollary III.

Chapter V

1. This link is also due to the fact, in itself revealing, that Foucault's «profound Nietzscheanism», referred to the problem of (bio)politics (one thinks as an example of certain passages of *La volonté de savoir*), takes on an unmistakable Schmittian colour. On this point see Berni 2005.

2. From his fundamental 1962 book on *Nietzsche et la philosophie*, up to his latest writings, in which he supports, with captivating arguments, the arcane «Spinoza–Nietzsche identity», Deleuze's thought is entirely unambiguous on this point. This is an issue worthy of further study, about which I limit myself to indicating the items in issue 47, 1995 of the review «Philosophie», monographically devoted to Deleuze, as well as other insightful contributions on Deleuze: see the 1994–7 issues of the review «Millepiani» and Fadini's introduction to Deleuze 1998.

3. Schmitt 1928: 76–7.

4. Ibid.

5. I refer to the recent debate inaugurated by Dogliani 1995 and carried forward by other Italian constitutionalists, such as Luciani 1995 and 1996, to which Palombella 1997 replied, in my opinion, convincingly.

6. Fioravanti 1998: 9–10.
7. Ibid.
8. See, further on in this volume, Corollary III. As Onfray 1997 has acutely observed, «the supporters of humanist religion, who are also the defenders of the mythology of the rights of man, exemplify the Realist option in the ancient dispute with Nominalists [. . .]. [But] their declaration of principle, even if it were generous, proud and magnificent – as in the cases of humanism and the rights of man – is worth nothing in the context of the real world, if the transition to action is impossible. Thus, humanism serves a cause contrary to the principle on which it is based: confined to the sole register of ethical biddings and moralising demands [. . .], this religion recreates Christianity in anthropological form», acting as «a practical smokescreen» (Part III, Chapter 1: *On the Individual*).
9. Miglio 1993: 19–20. Miglio's criticism is demystifying and liberating: «Ever since we've known the reasons for the political theology of Baroque absolutism, the (unfounded) principle has taken root whereby being "identical" is far better than being "different", and by virtue of its logical-political mechanisms this principle has become a dogma of *jus publicum Europaeum*, prompting a natural reaction in Western culture to recognise, for the first time, among its great unavailable natural rights, that of self-determination and democratic self-organisation of all the partnerships and groups that have become aware of their own diversity (and therefore non-standardisation)» (ibid.).
10. Ibid.
11. The consequences of the legitimacy of exercising the right of resistance and secession can be intuited. Lottieri 1993 has examined the issue with the same approach.
12. On the path opened up by Luhmann 1969. Concerning it, comparison is due, from a standpoint of politological realism, with Portinaro 1993, especially 140 ff.
13. See, further on in this volume, Corollary III.
14. Deleuze 1962: 64 ff. See on this point Fadini 1998: 103–46.

15. I refer once again on this point to Corollary III of this volume, dedicated to Jürgen Habermas's criticism of ethical universalism.
16. Thus M. Hauriou 1923: 285, with whom Schmitt in his work often finds himself in agreement: «The great evil that public law has suffered from for at least three-quarters of a century has been the abandonment of the classical theory of power: we no longer want to admit that what creates law is political power, whether or not this is understood as the power of the State.» See Beaud 1994: 9 ff. – who, however, in my opinion, is inconsistent in his proclaimed intention to situate himself in the classical tradition of European public law.
17. Negri 1992: 32–3.
18. On this point Böckenförde 1986 agrees, arguing rightly with Kriele 1981: 260 ff.

Corollary I

1. Among the most significant critical contributions on these points I limit myself to recalling Horkheimer 1938; Bense 1947; Rosso 1954.
2. See Koselleck 1959.
3. According to what he shows in his latest developments, the historiographic investigation undertaken in Italy by the work of Battista 1966.
4. Pintard 1943: 560.
5. Pintard 1943: ibid.
6. Montaigne, *Essais*, II, 5.
7. See on this point Schmitt's fundamental work (1950) about the transition from the moral-theological problems of the *justa causa belli* to the formal-juridical ones of the *bellum iustum* between states.
8. Friedrich 1949: 207.
9. Friedrich 1949: 205.
10. Borkenau 1934.
11. Friedrich 1949: 207.
12. Horkheimer 1938: 202.

13. Horkheimer 1938: 203.
14. I refer in particular to Schmitt's essay on Hamlet and Hecuba: Schmitt 1956.
15. The observation is Bonanate's in his review of the Italian edition of Schneider's book (Schneider 1970), which appeared in *Rivista di filosofia* 3, 1975.
16. See Negri 1970.
17. Thus Sedlmayr 1948, a work that, starting from the specific terrain of art history, offers notable insights also into the philosophical-cultural problem as a whole.
18. See Koselleck 1959, in Chapter I: «The political structure of Absolutism as premise for the Enlightenment».
19. Koselleck 1959, ibid. (in note).
20. Lenoble 1943: 544.
21. Thus Gregory 1967: 166.
22. More at length on this point, see my introduction to the Italian edition of Schnur 1963, now in Castrucci 1985: 37–50.
23. See the concept of *Abgrund* in Schnur 1963.
24. There re-emerge in relation to this the interpretive formats masterfully illustrated by Leo Strauss 1952.
25. It is the thesis that recurs in Charron, *Discours*, cit.
26. See Gargani 1977: 107, who reprises this topic in excellent fashion.
27. In this sense Popkin 1968, as well as Pacchi's monograph (Pacchi 1965).
28. Pacchi 1965: 13.
29. Nietzsche, *Menschliches, Allzumenschliches (II)*, in *KSA* 2, § 60: 579.
30. Nietzsche, *Menschliches, Allzumenschliches (I)*, in *KSA* 2, § 82: 86.
31. Schmitt 1938.
32. I refer, as is natural, to the work of Blumenberg 1960.
33. Schmitt 1934: 21–2.
34. Nietzsche, *Nachgelassene Fragmente 1885–1887*, in *KSA* 12, 9 [97]: 389–91.

Corollary II

1. Treated mainly in Schmitt 1938. It is true that the Hobbesian problem of *Veritas* gets closer treatment in other texts by Schmitt (see subsequent notes).
2. Schmitt 1963a: 121–3 (see above, Chapter V).
3. See Schmitt 1922, Chapter III of the same essay: 49 ff. See also id. 1963a: «The connection of political theories with theological dogmas of sin, which is particularly clear in Bossuet, Maistre, Bonald, Donoso Cortés and F. J. Stahl, but which is present just as intensely in countless other authors, is explained by the affinity of certain necessary presuppositions of thought. The fundamental theological dogma of the sinfulness of the world and of men leads – to the extent that theology has not yet dissolved into moral law or merely into pedagogy and dogma into mere discipline – just as the distinction of friend and enemy, to a division of men, to a "detachment", and makes impossible the undifferentiated optimism associated with a universal concept of man. Therefore the connection of the methodological presuppositions of theological and political thought seems clear» (64). On the theological roots of other legal concepts, among which is the very important one of representation, the political-philosophical literature is quite vast: it suffices to recall the investigations initiated by Voegelin's classic work (Voegelin 1952): the title, very significant, of Chapter II of this book is *Representation and Truth*. Interesting notes on the relationship between jurisprudence and theology in general can be found in Buddeberg's essay (Buddeberg 1937), especially part I: *Rechtswissenschaft und Theologie*. We also recall Marxen's old dissertation (Marxen 1937).
4. *Auctoritas* answers the question about 'who', *Veritas* about 'what': the latter is *Scriptura sacra* providing the normative content, but that consigns to secular history the results of the activity of decision. As Schmitt claims, Locke «does not see that law does not say *to whom* it gives authority. Yet it is not that anyone can execute and

implement any possible juridical norm. But this last as norm of decision states only *how* it must be decided, not also *who* should decide. Anyone may appeal to the correctness of the content, if there were not a last claim. But the last claim does not derive from the norm» (Schmitt 1922: 43–4).

5. As can be understood even now, our analysis of the concept of political theology deliberately refrains from considering the German debate of the 1960s and 1970s on the so-called «new political theology» (J. B. Metz, J. Moltmann, etc.), which moreover appears flawed by a clear misunderstanding of the classical concept of p. th., which is that brought to light by the Hobbes–Schmitt line of interpretation. This debate takes place purely *innertheologisch*. See, however, about all this, the informed survey of Ruini 1980, who notes that Moltmann intends p.th. as «critical of the "civil religion" that had been theorised in the old (*sic!*) forms of political theology and crops up under different guises, open or dissembled, in all political regimes (including atheist socialisms). It is a politicisation of religion in the sense of reason of state and is useful for the symbolic integration and a mythic-sacral consolidation of a society» (Ruini: 914). The considerations of Metz, Moltmann, etc. can simply be traced back to the definition of p.th.[2]. But here, Alberico Gentili instructs: «Silete theologi munere alieno!»

6. This was the viewpoint of European political decisionism already during the seventeenth-century «*manieristischer Ordnungsversuch*», according to Schnur's meaningful expression (Schnur 1963, especially Chapter IV).

7. Schmitt 1963a: p. 39.

8. According to the reference to the famous passage of St Paul's *Epistle to the Romans* (Ch. XIII): «Omnis anima potestatibus sublimioribus subdita sit: non est enim potestas nisi a Deo».

9. Concerning the difference between the sacred doctrine of authority and the doctirne of divine right, the reference is to A. Passerin d'Entrèves 1962: 258 ss.

10. Schmitt 1922: 42: «In jeder Umformung liegt eine auctoritatis interpositio». Schmitt's arguments against authors as Kelsen, Krabbe, Preuß and Wolzendorff proceed in this rigorously personalistic sense, occupying almost the entire Chapter II of *Politische Theologie*.

11. Schmitt 1928: 83–4, on whom Voegelin's criticism should be considered (Voegelin 1931: 89 ff.) But Burdeau's observations should also be considered: «Nous avons des expériences quotidiennes qui nous sont présentées à un rythme accéléré où le peuple adhère à des actes imputés à sa volonté sans qu'il ait participé à leur rédaction. J'étais en Egypte lorsque la Constitution a été adoptée; j'ai vu que l'on mettait des haut-parleurs sur les lampadaires et le lendemain matin le peuple a été convié à entendre la Constitution dont on lui affirma qu'il était l'auteur. Il en fut si bien convaincu qu'il s'est acclamé lui-même. Avec une société de masse c'est ce que l'on peut attendre aujourd'hui d'un procédé démocratique; ce n'est peut-être pas rationnellement ce que l'on pourrait en souhaiter, mais c'est en fait ce qui est possible. Dans un match de football, il n'y a jamais que deux fois onze garçons qui envoient des coups de pieds dans un ballon, mais il y a cependant 50.000 spectateurs qui jouent et qui gagnent. Ils ont participé. Je ne me fais pas d'illusion, entre nous, sur la qualité de cette participation, mais j'ai très sincèrement, quoiqu'avec quelque regret, la conviction que c'est le seul type de participation auquel nous puissions prétendre aujourd'hui» (Burdeau 1965: 43–4).

12. For the debate in German juridical literature, see Böckenförde 1991: 58–66.

13. Marx 1858, on the free development of the collective intellect.

14. Bloch 1918.

15. Benjamin 1921: 511–12.

16. St Paul, *Second letter to the Thessalonians*, 2, 6 ss. In this enigmatic passage St Paul mentions the future advent of the Antichrist, where *katechon* indicates what restrains the Antichrist from fully manifesting himself, bursting

apocalyptically into human history. «You know» – says Paul to the Thessalonians – «what it is that restrains him from manifesting himself in his time. Because the *mysterium iniquitatis* is already at work, but the force that has held him until now must be done away with» (ibid.). For Schmitt (1950: 28 ff.), who in *Der Nomos der Erde* interprets these passages of St Paul in a neo-gnostic key, the most obvious historical example of the action exerted by this «braking force» (*Aufhalter*) was the Christian medieval *respublica*, the political form of the empire. «Empire means here the historical power that succeeds in *restraining* the advent of the Antichrist and the end of the present Aeon» (29). Important considerations are to be found in Taubes' book, which remains one of the most stimulating treatises on Pauline philosophical-theological issues as a whole (Taubes 1993).

17. Thus Pasqualucci 1978: 588. In this context, Rumpf's essay (Rumpf 1976), and, in Italian literature, Desideri 1980, should be considered.

18. C. Schmitt, *Das Zeitalter der Neutralisierungen und Entpolitisierungen* (1929), in id. 1963a: 93. Schmitt goes on to say: «Every genuine revival with its return to the basic principle of its nature, every authentic returning to the *principle* [. . .] appears, before the ease and comfort of the status quo, as a cultural or social nothing. They are all phenomena that grow silently and in the shadows and, in their early beginnings, a historian or sociologist would not be able to see other than nothing [. . .]. The order of human affairs springs from the strength of a sound conscience. *Ab integro nascitur ordo*» (ibid. pp. 94–5).

19. The problem is present, in all its meaning also political, in the later Schmitt, who in *Politische Theologie II* observes: «Gnostic dualism poses a God of love, a God estranged from the world, like God the Redeemer against the righteous God, the lord and creator of this wicked world. Both act if not in an active mutual enmity, certainly in an irreconcilable estrangement, a kind of risky cold war whose enmity may be more intense than enmity manifested

openly and almost naively on the battlefield. [. . .] But the essential structural problem of Gnostic dualism [. . .] is ineradicably immanent in any world in which a need for change and renewal presents itself. Enmity among men cannot be eliminated by prohibiting wars between States waged in the old style, by propagating a world revolution and trying to transform world politics into world police. The concept of revolution, unlike those of reform, revision and evolution, implies a hostile dispute. The lord of a world to be changed, or of a wrong world (whose need for change is recognised, without its wanting to submit to it, indeed with its opposing it) and the liberator, who produces a new changed world, can obviously not be good friends.» Thus Schmitt 1970: 119–21.

20. Pasqualucci 1978: 596, note 9.

21. See Blumenberg 1974. Schmitt observes that «for Blumenberg secularisation is a category of historical injustice. He tries to unmask it as such, hoping to transcend its translations and transformations in what he configures as the legitimacy of modernity. With his book *Die Legitimität der Neuzeit* Blumenberg wields a juridical banner. His challenge appears all the greater when one consider that the term "legitimacy" for over a century has indicated the monopoly of dynastic legitimacy, in the continued recourse to concepts such as duration, antiquity, ancestry and tradition, in the name of a "historic" justification of the past and of a "historical school of law" whose progressive and revolutionary opponents reproached it for having served to justify the injustice of today with the injustice of yesterday. Now it seems easy to overturn anything, thanks to an unprecedented self-justification of the new» (Schmitt 1970: 111). It should be remembered that Blumenberg then inserted in the second enlarged and revised edition of his book on the legitimacy of modernity, a chapter in which he subjects Schmitt's theses in *Politische Theologie I* and *II* to scrutiny: the title is *Säkularisierung und Selbstbehauptung*: See Blumenberg 1974, Chapter VIII.

22. See further, § 6, point IV.
23. Schmitt 1970: 92. Thomas Hobbes, under this interpretation, seems one who had «brought» the Reformation «to completion», exhausting the possibilities of *jus reformandi* and paving the way for those – modern and uncontrollable – of the *jus revolutionis*: See Schmitt 1965, on whom Schmitt 1970: 121.
24. Schmitt 1970: 110.
25. Ibid. p. 98.
26. «... zwischen denen sogar enharmonische Verwechselungen zulässig und sinnvoll werden» (ibid. p. 101).
27. «Das ist nur eine Frage der richtigen Temperierung der Instrumente» (ibid.).
28. Schmitt 1958: 451, italics mine. Thus Schmitt continues: «The transformation of law into legality was immediately followed by the transformation of legality into a weapon of civil war. This too was not a German discovery, Lenin had already proclaimed it with full awareness and emphasis. His work *Extremism, Childhood Disease of Communism* (1920), is in this respect such a crucial document that any discussion on the issue of legality, without familiarity with that work, seems anachronistic. Lenin states: 'Revolutionaries who do not understand the need to connect illegal forms of struggle with *all* (the emphasis is Lenin's own) legal ones, are clearly bad revolutionaries.' And again: «In a novel by Bertolt Brecht, at the end the gangster boss orders his followers: work must be legal. Legality winds up here as the password of a gangster. It had begun as ambassador of the divinity of reason» (ibid.).
29. Schmitt 1970: 101, note 1.
30. On the sixteenth-century European genesis of this ethic, I refer to Castrucci 1981.
31. See above all Heidegger 1950. On the delicate theoretical relationship between Schmitt's and Heidegger's metaphysics, see the work of Graf von Krockow 1958, as well as – it too from an openly critical viewpoint – Löwith 1960, expanded version, about the problem of the

relationship between Schmitt and Heidegger, of an essay of 1935.

32. Thus Staff (1981: 724) observes that «since in the modern era there is no general consensus about absolute values, in that it is reason itself which stands as individualised, *we must then borrow an absolute from theology*, to whose conceptual apparatus the absoluteness of a divine truth traditionally belongs, which can legitimise everything. When Schmitt transfers the concept of the truth of Christian theology onto the terrain of the political, calling this transfer secularisation, secularisation then reveals itself above all as an act of conceptual force, enacted to replace the reality of pluralism with the ideology of a substantial unity» (italics mine).

33. See above, note 16. «Eine Kraft quae tenet», as described in the paragraph of *Nomos der Erde* dedicated to the Christian medieval empire as a «braking force» (*Aufhalter*), *katechon*. Thus Schmitt 1950: 29–30: «The empire of the Christian Middle Ages lasted for as long as there remained alive the idea of *katechon*. I do not believe that the original Christian faith can have in general an image of history different from that of *katechon*. Faith in a braking force able to restrain the end of the world lays down the only bridges that from the eschatological paralysis of every human occurrence leads to a grandiose historical power like that of the Christian empire of the Germanic kings. The authority of the Church fathers and writers such as Tertullian, St Jerome, Lactantius Firmianus, and the Christian continuation of Sibylline prophecies, concur that only the *Imperium Romanum* and its Christian continuation explain the existence of the aeon and its steadfast resistance to the overwhelming power of evil.»

34. Thus Girard 1972 in the first chapter of his book, which treats the concept of sacrifice.

35. Schmitt 1926: 41–2, italics mine. Tommissen 1975: 496 called attention to this passage of Schmitt's, though without examining its meaning any further. On the

controversial topic of Schmitt's «political Catholicism», I refer to Kodalle 1973: espec. 109.

36. «Political unity is, by its essence, decisive unity, it matters not from what forces it draws its ultimate psychic motivations. It either exists or does not. If it exists, it is the supreme unity, that is the one that decides in the decisive instance» (Schmitt 1963a: 44). According to Schmitt this confirms the entire inadequacy of the associationist theories of the State, «whose acuity is exhausted in polemics against the previous overestimations of the State, against its "superiority" and "personality", against its '"monopoly" of supreme unity, while it remains unclear what, in general, political unity itself should be» (ibid.).

37. In Leo Spitzer's sense (Spitzer 1963).

38. See Schmitt 1970: 116 ff., 122 ff.

39. J. Donne, *Sermons*, vol. II: 170.

40. M. Mersenne, *Harmonie*, and in particular id., *Vérité*: 419 ff.

41. Schnur 1963: 73–4.

42. Spitzer 1963: 99–100.

43. Schmitt 1967.

44. Schmitt 1970: 126.

Corollary III

1. See Habermas 1992, esp. Chapter I. See further id. 1996. By mere way of example: «Our problematic situation [. . .] takes for granted the existence of a convenient, non-problematic medium [*zweckgemässig*] such as decreed, coercive law [. . .]. Especially since in the complex societies of modernity (whether Asian or European) there seems to be no other functional equivalent able to absolve the same integrative functions as positive law. The artificiality of these types of norms – together liberal and coercive – has also been able to generate an abstract form of civic solidarity [*staatsbürgerlich*] pledging to each other outsiders who want to continue to remain such» (Habermas 1998: 180).

2. Habermas 1992: 104 ff. (Habermas's italics).
3. He goes on to say: «Moral and juridical questions refer clearly to the same problems: that is, how justified norms can legitimately order between them interpersonal relations or coordinate actions, how conflicting actions can be resolved by consensus against the background of inter-subjectively recognised rules and normative principles. Moral and legal questions nevertheless refer to the same problems in respectively different forms» (ibid.).
4. For an exact, even historical-philological reconstruction, of the topic, see lastly Marini 1998.
5. I refer essentially to the essays contained in Habermas 1996.
6. Habermas 1996: 219.
7. Barcellona 1994: 40–1. Such as to be able to conclude in drastic fashion that «in fact, the exercise of so-called rational competence coincides with the exercise of a manipulative competence» (47).
8. On which Lübbe's timely criticisms must be seen (see Lübbe 1994).
9. As already proposed seventy years ago by Kelsen 1944.
10. Schmitt 1963a: 55 and 94: «. . . So ist das kein Krieg der Menschheit, sondern ein Krieg, für den eine bestimmte Macht gegenüber seinem Kriegsgegner einen universalen Begriff zu okkupieren sucht, ähnlich wie man Frieden, Gerechtigkeit, Fortschritt und Zivilisation mißbrauchen kann, um sie für sich zu vindizieren und dem Feinde abzusprechen. "Menschheit" ist ein besonders brauchbares ideologisches Instrument [. . .]. Wir kennen das geheime Gesetz dieses Vokabulariums und wissen, daß heute der schrecklichste Krieg im Namen des Friedens. . . und die schrecklichste Unmenschlichkeit im Namen der Menschlichkeit vollzogen wird.»
11. *Kants Idee des ewigen Friedens – aus dem historischen Abstand von 200 Jahren*, § IV.
12. «*a*) die Politik der Menschenrechte dient der Durchsetzung von Normen, die Teil einer universalistischen Moral sind; *b*) da moralische Urteile dem Code von "Gut" und "Böse"

gehorchen, zerstört die negative moralische Bewertung (eines politischen Opponenten bzw.) eines Kriegsgegners die rechtlich institutionalisierte Begrenzung (der politischen Auseinandersetzung bzw.) des militärischen Kampfes» (Habermas 1996: p. 221).

13. In this regard, we find instructive the warning – which rings like a real call to order – that in another place Habermas addresses to Western intellectuals who identify with the leftist project of government: «Western intellectuals should be careful not to confuse *their* self-critical discourse on Eurocentric prejudices with debates that *others* undertake with them» (Habermas 1996: 181, Habermas's italics). Who these 'others' are is easily understood after what Habermas affirmed shortly before about the need to redimension (which means: isolate, expunge from the theoretical debate) that «hermeneutics of suspicion» that developed in Germany in the wake of Heidegger and Schmitt, in the dual form of a critique of reason and a critique of power (ibid. p. 223). In these calls to order addressed to *clercs* the left we glimpse an entirely political call (with a sectarian and in no way ethical-discursive tone) to close ranks, not unworthy of some – even well known to Habermas – forms of socialism.

14. «While the first premise is false, the second premise – if it is referred to the politics of human rights – suggests an erroneous presupposition» (Habermas 1996: 221).

15. «It is no coincidence that only in these early constitutional texts do human rights take on a concrete form. Here they appear as fundamental rights guaranteed in the framework of a national legal system. Nevertheless, they seem to have a dual character: while as constitutional norms they have positive validity, as rights due to every human person they also maintain a superpositive validity» (ibid.).

16. «The core of truth [of Schmitt's critique] lies in the fact that an *immediate* [*unvermittelte*] moralisation of law and politics would effectively crush those "protected areas" [*Schutzzonen*] of law that we [...] want to safeguard for

subjects of rights [*Rechtspersonen*]. It is however mistaken to believe that to avoid this moralisation we must liberate (or make a clean sweep of) the international politics of law and the law of morality» (Habermas 1996: 233).

17. Habermas 1996: 222, Habermas's italics.
18. «In jedem Fall bleibt. . . der moralische Universalismus, der Kant bei seinem Vorhaben geleitet hat, die maßstab-bildende Intuition [eines] moralisch-praktischen Selbst-verständnis der Moderne» (Habermas 1996: 219).
19. Habermas 1996: 231.
20. «What on earth is a "crime against humanity"? Are there perhaps crimes against love?»: so Schmitt 1991: 113, cit. in Habermas 1996: 228–9.
21. Schmitt 1928: 226 ff.
22. As Habermas himself recognises, «this is an ambiguity that has generated more than one of bewilderment in philosophical discussion. According to some, the statute of human rights should be placed midway between moral law and positive law. According to others, human rights should – maintaining the same content – have the status of both moral and legal rights: a sort of 'valid pre-state law, but not however automatically in force. [. . .] These embarrassed formulations seem to suggest that constitutent legislator should simply pave over with positive law moral norms given *a priori*' (Habermas 1996: 221). But the path taken by Habermas for overcoming this dilemma: to declare fundamental rights (and with them human rights) already as such juridically finalised, estab-lishing a gradualist genealogical development starting from the subjective State rights of classical law (almost as if there were no 'leaps' in the logical development of the rule of law and the human rights of the universalist cosmopolis) is even less convincing and conceals unac-ceptable conceptual approximations.
23. Habermas 1996: 223, Habermas's italics.
24. Ibid. In fact «being part of a democratic juridical system, fundamental rights too enjoy (like all other jurdical norms) an ideal validity of their own [*Gültigkeit*]. In the

sense that they are not only effectively applicable [. . .], but they can also claim legitimacy since liable to rational justification» (222).

25. Guilty, in Habermas's own words, of seeing in human rights «the expression of a specifically Western reason, rooted in Platonism. Victim of an "abstractive prejudice", this reason would place itself outside the limits of its original context and, in so doing, outside of a merely local validity of its would-be universal criteria. Every tradition, image of the world or culture should have inscribed in themselves their respective (and incommensurable) criteria for judging truth and the falsehood» (Habermas, *Zur Legitimation durch Menschenrechte*, in id. 1998: 181).

26. Or consensus reached by an «overlapping» of the moral principles that characterise different cultures, in the belief that these principles are basically homogenous, since traceable to a common core of moral intuitions on which the great prophetic religions of the planet (significantly universalist) converge *ab origine*.

27. Habermas 1998: 190–1, italics mine.

28. In this sense the essays gathered in the book edited by Shute and Hurley 1993 are representative. Rorty's essay is worthy of attention for his discussion of the in favour of an openly anti-foundationalist theory of human rights expressed by the Argentinian E. Rabossi, for whom «the world has changed, and the phenomenon of human rights makes obsolete and irrelevant the search for their philosophical foundation» (ibid. p. 132). One can only say that, even if (and willingly granted) metaphysical foundationalism no longer poses an inescapable destiny for ethical theory, the purely pragmatic type of justification that Rorty proposes remains very weak. Instead Rorty's following reflection is worthy of attention: «The moral educator will no longer be given the task of responding to the rational egoist when he wonders: "Why should I have a morality?", But rather what to answer the much more frequent question, "Why should I care about a stranger, a person with whom I have no family ties and whose

customs bother me?", the answer traditionally given to the second question is: "Because the bonds of kinship and customs are morally irrelevant, that is irrelevant to the obligations deriving from the fact of recognising their membership in our own species." This answer has never been very convincing, for the simple reason that it takes for granted that it is the very crux of the problem: whether, that is, the simple fact of belonging to the species can actually be considered a valid surrogate of one's closest relationships» (ibid. p. 150). It should be noted, however, that Rabossi's theoretical position appears entirely superficial, in his insistence that a «human rights culture» is by now «an undeniable reality», accepted on a planetary scale even at the institutional level (a recurrent motif in Habermas himself), is sufficient reason to definitively exonerate the philosopher from asking further questions.

29. «The essential content of moral principles embodied in international law» as Habermas himself frequently claims, «is in keeping with the normative substance of the great prophetic doctrines and metaphysical interpretations affirmed in universal history» (Habermas 1990: 20).

30. In his constant preoccupation not to retrace the aporetic paths of classic natural law, which Habermas himself recognises is completely «ambiguous»: «It is an ambiguity that has generated more than one disconcertedness in philosophical discussion. According to some, the statute of human rights should be placed midway between moral law and positive law. According to others, human rights should present itself – maintaining the same content – both as both moral and juridical rights: a sort of "pre-State" valid law, but not for that automatically in force» (Habermas 1996: 221).

31. «Grundrechte regeln [. . .] Materien von solcher Allgemeinheit, daß moralische Argumente *zu ihrer Begründung hinreichen*. Das sind Argumente, die begründen, warum die Gewährleistung solcher Regeln im gleichmäßigen Interesse aller Personen in ihrer Eigenschaft als Personen

überhaupt liegen, warum sie also gleichermaßen gut sind für *jedermann*». So Habermas, *Kants Idee des ewigen Friedens*, in Habermas 1996: 223, Habermas's italics.

32. «Der wahre Kern besteht darin, daß eine *unvermittelte* Moralisierung von Recht und Politik tatsächlich jene Schutzzonen durchbricht, die wir [. . .] gewahrt wissen wollen [. . .] Tatsächlich würde sich in der internationalen Arena eine *unvermittelte* Moralisierung der Politik schädlich auswirken» (ibid., in Habermas 1996: 233–4, Habermas's italics).

33. Habermas 1996: 235.

34. Which show us that «those who establish a certain value impose at all times, *eo ipso*, a non-value. The meaning of this imposition of values is the annihilation of non-values» (Schmitt 1963b: 80–1, n. 49).

35. «Das Weltbürgerrecht ist eine Konsequenz der Rechtsstaatsidee.» So Habermas, *Kants Idee des ewigen Friedens*, in Habermas 1996: 234.

36. But instead it is true that «l'absence d'une règle neutre pour resoudre les conflits entre les hommes est une experience inévitable à laquelle personne ne peut se soustraire. Il y a toujours le risque – et exister signifie l'accepter – que les autres ne reconnaissent pas ma différence par rapport à eux. [. . .] Il y a toujours la possibilité qu'on doive combattre pour sa propre identité.» Furthermore, «la théorie est "pure" en tant qu'elle se place à distance de tout ce qui est enraciné, non répétable, non réproductible, territorialisé, bref, tout ce qui nous engage à prendre position. [. . .] La polarité ami-ennemi perce à travers la neutralité de l'espace public dépolitisé gouverné par les lois et les appareils administratifs. [. . .] Le problème politique de notre époque réside dans cette absence d'ennemi, dans ce rejet de la relation ami-ennemi comme intelligible.» (Belohradsky 1988: 55, 44, 57).

37. The responsibility for this 'veering' is undoubtedly Habermas's strong tendency to be an interpreter – and one in the forefront – of the leading political tendencies in Western 'leftist government' circles, which indicates

– it is impossible to deny – a great 'political' dexterity of adaptation and more than a hint of opportunism. But on this point everything has already been said and the issue has become devoid of theoretical interest. On the drop in tension in Frankfurt criticism I will only recall C. Türcke's pungent observations (Türcke 1992).

38. I use these terms («tyranny» over the «system of values») in the specific sense attributed to them in C. Schmitt's essay (Schmitt 1967). The truth is that «no one can evaluate without devaluing, increasing in value, and endorsing. Those who establish values take a stand against non-values»: «Niemand kann werten ohne abzuwerten, aufzuwerten und zu verwerten. Wer Werte setzt, hat sich damit gegen Unwerte abgesetzt» (Schmitt 1967: 58). From all this we can easily understand the reason (from the «inherent logic of values») why the politics of the rights of man *necessarily* produces discrimination against one's opponent: «Any regard for one's enemy falls away, indeed turns into a non-value, when the battle against this enemy is a battle for *supreme values*. Non-value has no right before value, and no price is too high for the imposition of supreme value» («Jede Rücksicht auf den Gegner entfällt, ja sie wird zum Unwert, wenn der Kampf gegen diesen Gegner ein Kampf um die *höchsten Werte* ist. Der Unwert hat kein Recht gegenüber dem Wert, und für die Durchsetzung des höchsten Wertes ist kein Preis zu hoch» (ibid. p. 61, italics mine).

39. «Der Begriff der Menschheit schließt den Begriff des Feindes aus» (Schmitt 1963a: 54–5). But, to the extent that it subsumes political relationships under the categories of 'good' and 'evil', it transforms the belligerent enemy into «that inhuman monster that cannot only be *defeated*, but must be permanently *destroyed*» [«unmenschliche Scheusal, das nicht nur abgewehrt, sondern definitiv vernichtet werden muß»] (ibid. p. 120, italics mine). The lack of understanding of the anthropological roots of the 'political' ends up inevitably amplifying violence. This belief is clearly expressed and argued in fundamental

studies of authors such as René Girard (see Girard 1972 and 1978).

40. See the quote here in the epigraph. A reference that is found today mercilessly photographed in the caustic pages of Hans Magnus Enzensberger: «Typical of the West is the rhetoric of universalism. [. . .] Universalism knows no difference between what is close and what is far away: it is absolute and abstract. The concept of human rights requires on everyone obligations that, in principle, know no borders. [. . .] However, since all of our options for action are limited, the gap between desire and reality becomes increasingly deep. It soon crossed the threshold of factual hypocrisy. Universalism thus reveals itself to be a moral trap» (Enzensberger 1993: § IX).

Bibliography

Philosophical Sources

Al-Ghazali (*Tahafut*): *Tahafut al-falasifa* [*Incoherence of the Philosophers*], ed. M. Bouyges, Beyrouth: Imprimerie Catholique, 1927. English translation by S. A. Kamali, Lahore: Pakistan Philosophical Congress, 1958.

Aquinas (*Summa Theologica*): *Sancti Thomae de Aquino Summa theologica*, eds Domenicani italiani, Florence: Salani, 1966.

Aquinas (*Quaestiones disputatae*): *Quaestiones disputatae de potentia Dei: Quaestiones I–III*, in Aquinas, *Opera omnia*, vol. III, Stuttgart-Bad Cannstatt: Frommann-Holzboog, 1980.

Aristotle (*Met.*): *Aristotle's Metaphysics, A Revised Text with Introduction and Commentary*, translated by W. D. Ross, Oxford: Oxford University Press, 1924.

Charron, P. (*Discours*): *Discours chrestien qu'il n'est permis ny loisible au subiect pour quelque cause et raison que ce soit de se liguer, bander et rebeller contre son Roy*, Paris: Le Clerc, 1606.

Donne, J. (*Sermons*): *Sermons on the Psalms and Gospels*, ed. E. M. Simpson, Berkeley: University of California Press, 1955.

Duns Scotus, J. (*Ox.*): *Commentaria oxoniensia ad IV libros Magistri Sententiarum*, ed. M. Fernandez Garcia, I–II, Ad Claras Aquas prope Florentiam: Typ. Collegii St Bonaventurae, 1912–14.

Hobbes, Th. (*E. W.*): *The English Works of Thomas Hobbes of Malmesbury*, ed. W. Molesworth, London: J. Bohn, 1839–5.

Leibniz, G. W. (*Nova Methodus*): *Nova methodus discendae docendaeque Jurisprudentiae*, Halle: Krug, 1748.

Leibniz, G. W. (*Theodicea*): *Essais de Théodicée*, in: *Die philosophischen Schriften von G. W. von Leibnitz*, ed. C. I. Gerhardt, VI, Hildesheim: Olms, 1965.

Mersenne, M. o.f.m. (*Vérité*): *La vérité des sciences, contre les Septiques ou Pyrrhoniens*, Paris: chez Toussainct du Bray, 1626.

Mersenne, M. o.f.m. (*Harmonie*): *Harmonie universelle*, Paris: chez Sebastien Cramoisy, 1636–7.

Montaigne (de), M. (*Essais*): *Essais*, in M. de Montaigne, *Oeuvres complètes*, eds A Thibaudet and M. Rat, Paris: Gallimard, 1962.

Nietzsche, F. (*KSA*): *Sämtliche Werke. Kritische Studienausgabe*, eds G. Colli and M. Montinari, Berlin and New York: De Gruyter, 1967 ff.

Ockham, W. (*Quodlibeta*): *Quodlibeta septem*, in J. C. Wey (ed.), *Guillelmi de Ockham Opera philosophica et theologica ad fidem codicum manuscriptorum edita*, vol. IX, New York: St Bonaventure, 1980.

Ockham, W. (*TcB*): *Tractatus contra Benedictum*, in R. F. Bennett and H. S. Offler (eds), *Guillelmi de Ockham Opera politica*, vol. III, Manchester: Manchester University Press, 1956.

Petrus de Tarantasia (*Sent.*): *Commentaria in IV libros Sententiarum Petri Lombardi*, I–IV, Tolosae: apud Arnaldum Colomerium, 1649–52, Ridgewood, NJ: Gregg Press, 1964.

Rousseau, J.-J. (*CS*): *Le contrat social*, in J.-J. Rousseau, *The Political Writings of Jean-Jacques Rousseau*, edited from the original MSS and authentic editions by C. E. Vaughan, Oxford: Blackwell, 1962.

Spinoza, B. (*Eth.*): *Ethica*, in B. Spinoza, *Opera*, ed. C. Gebhardt, vol. II, pp. 41–308, Heidelberg: Carl Winter Verlag, 1925.

Spinoza, B. (*TP*): *Tractatus politicus*, ibid. vol. III, pp. 269–360.

Spinoza, B. (*TTP*): *Tractatus theologico-politicus*, ibid. vol. III, pp. 1–267.

Bibliography

Critical Literature

Agamben, G. (1993), 'Bartleby, or On Contingency', in G. Agamben (1999), *Potentialities: Collected Essays in Philosophy*, Stanford: Stanford University Press.

Amsterdamski, S. (1978), sub voce 'Convenzione', *Enciclopedia Einaudi*, vol. III, Turin: Einaudi.

Atger, F. (1906), *Essai sur l'histoire des doctrines du contrat social*, Nîmes: Imprimerie Cooperative 'La laborieuse'.

Bannach, K. (1975), *Die Lehre von der doppelten Macht Gottes bei Wilhelm von Ockham*, Wiesbaden: Steiner.

Barcellona, P. (1994), *Dallo Stato sociale allo Stato immaginario*, Turin: Bollati Boringhieri.

Battista, A. M. (1966), *Alle origini del pensiero politico libertino. Montaigne e Charron*, Milan: Giuffrè.

Baudry, L. (1958), *Lexique philosophique de Guillaume d'Ockham: Études des notions fondamentales*, Paris: Lethielleux.

Beaud, O. (1994), *La puissance de l'Etat*, Paris: Presses Universitaires de France.

Beaufret, J. (1973), *Dialogue avec Heidegger*, 3 vols, Paris: Minuit.

Becchi, P. (1995), 'La lunga ombra del Leviatano. Il carteggio inedito tra Carl Schmitt e Karl-Heinz Ilting', *Diritto e cultura. Archivio di filosofia e sociologia*, 1, 1995, pp. 115 ff.

Belaval, Y. (1983), 'Leibniz lecteur de Spinoza', *Archives de philosophie*, 46, pp. 531 ff.

Belohradsky, V. (1988), 'La modernité comme passion du neutre', *Le messager européen*, 2, pp. 23 ff.

Benjamin, W. (1921), 'Theologisch-politisches Fragment', in W. Benjamin (1955), *Schriften*, eds T. W. Adorno and G. Adorno, vol. I, Frankfurt a.M.: Suhrkamp.

Bense, M. (1947), 'Über den Essay', *Merkur*, 3, pp. 414 ff.

Berni, S. (2005), *Nietzsche e Foucault. Corporeità e potere in una critica radicale alla modernità*, Milan: Giuffrè.

Biuso, A. G. (1991), 'Nietzsche e Spinoza', *Archivio di storia della cultura*, IV, pp. 93 ff.

Bloch, E. (1918), *Geist der Utopie*, München: Duncker & Humblot.

Blondel, M. (1916), 'L'anticartésianisme de Malebranche', *Revue de Métaphysique et de Morale*.

Blumenberg, H. (1960), *Paradigmen zu einer Metaphorologie*, Frankfurt a.M.: Suhrkamp.

Blumenberg, H. (1969), 'Paradigmen zu einer Metaphorologie', *Archiv für Begriffsgeschichte*, VI.

Blumenberg, H. (1974), *Die Legitimität der Neuzeit*, Frankfurt a.M.: Suhrkamp.

Böckenförde, E.-W. (1986), *Die verfassunggebende Gewalt des Volkes – ein Grenzbegriff des Verfassungsrechte*, Frankfurt a.M.: Suhrkamp.

Böckenförde, E.-W. (1991), 'Das Bild vom Menschen in der Perspektive der heutigen Rechtsordnung', in E.-W. Böckenförde, *Recht, Staat, Freiheit. Studien zur Rechtsphilosophie, Staatstheorie und Verfassungsgeschichte*, Frankfurt a.M.: Suhrkamp.

Borkenau, F. (1934), *Der Übergang vom feudalen zum bürgerlichen Weltbild*, Paris: Alcan.

Breuer, S. (1984), 'Nationalstaat und pouvoir constituant bei Sieyès und Carl Schmitt', *Archiv für Rechts- und Sozialphilosophie*, 4, pp. 495 ff.

Buddeberg, K. Th. (1936–7), 'Descartes und der politische Absolutismus', *Archiv für Rechts- und Sozialphilosophie*, XXX.

Buddeberg, K. Th. (1937), 'Gott und Souverän. Über die Führung des Staates im Zusammenhang rechtlichen und religiösen Denkens', *Archiv des öffentlichen Rechts*, XXVIII.

Burdeau, G. (1965), *Le plan comme mythe*, in *La planification comme processus de decision*, Cahiers de la Fondation Nationale des Sciences politiques, n. 140, Paris: Librairie Armand Colin, pp. 35 ff.

Castrucci, E. (1981), *Ordine convenzionale e pensiero decisionista. Saggio sui presupposti intellettuali dello Stato moderno nel Seicento francese*, Milan: Giuffrè.

Castrucci, E. (1985), *La forma e la decisione. Studi critici*, Milan: Giuffrè.

Clark, D. W. (1978), 'Ockham on Human and Divine Freedom', *Franciscan Studies*, XXXVIII, pp. 122 ff.

Bibliography

Corwin, E. S. (1928–9), 'The "Higher Law", Background of American Constitutional Law', *Harvard Law Review*, pp. 625 ff.

Courtenay, W. J. (1973), 'The Critique of Natural Causality in the Mutakallimun and Nominalism', *The Harvard Theological Review*, vol. 66, pp. 77 ff.

Courtenay, W. J. (1974), 'Nominalism and Late Medieval Religion', in H. A. Oberman and Ch. Trinkhaus (eds), *The Pursuit of Holiness in the Late Medieval and Renaissance Religion*, Leiden: E. J. Brill, pp. 26 ff.

Courtenay, W. J. (1984), *Covenant and Causality in Medieval Thought*, London: Variorum Reprints.

Courtenay, W. J. (1985), 'The Dialectic of Omnipotence in the High and Late Middle Ages', in T. Rudavsky (ed.), *Divine Omniscience and Omnipotence in Medieval Philosophy*, Dordrecht, Boston and Lancaster: Reidel, 243 ff.

Deleuze, G. (1962), *Nietzsche et la philosophie*, Paris: Presses Universitaires de France.

Deleuze, G. (1978), *Spinoza et le problème de l'expression*, Paris: Minuit.

Del Noce, A. (1965), *Riforma cattolica e filosofia moderna. I. Cartesio*, Bologna: il Mulino.

Desideri, F. (1980), *Walter Benjamin: il tempo e le forme*, Rome: Editori Riuniti.

Dogliani, M. (1995), 'Potere costituente e revisione costituzionale', *Quaderni costituzionali*, vol. 15, n. 1, pp. 7 ff.

Droetto, A. (1980), 'Introduzione' to B. Spinoza, *Tractatus theologico-politicus*, eds A. Droetto and E. Giancotti Boscherini, Turin: Einaudi, pp. XI ff.

Enzensberger, H. M. (1993), *Aussichten auf den Bürgerkrieg*, Frankfurt a.M.: Suhrkamp.

Fadini, U. (1998), *Deleuze plurale. Per un pensiero nomade*, Bologna: Pendragon.

Figgis, J. N. (1934), *The Divine Right of Kings*, Cambridge: Cambridge University Press.

Fioravanti, M. (1998), *Costituzione e popolo sovrano*, Bologna: il Mulino.

Friedrich, H. (1949), *Montaigne*, Bern: Francke.

Gargani, A. G. (1977), 'Scienza e forme di vita', *Nuova Corrente*, 72–3, pp. 107 ff.

Gazzolo, T. (2014), *La scrittura della legge. Saggio su Montesquieu*, Naples: Jovene.

Gilson, J. (1948), *L'être et l'essence*, Paris: Vrin.

Gilson, J. (1952), *La philosophie au Moyen-Age*, Paris: Payot.

Girard, R. (1972), *La violence et le sacré*, Paris: Grasset.

Girard, R. (1978), *Des choses cachées depuis la fondation du monde. Recherches avec J.-M. Oughourlian et G. Lefort*, Paris: Grasset.

Gregory, T. (1967), 'La saggezza scettica di Pierre Charron', *De Homine*, pp. 67 ff.

Gregory, T. (1982), 'La tromperie divine', *Studi medievali*, XIII, pp. 517 ff.

Grua, G. (1953), *Jurisprudence universelle et théodicée selon Leibniz*, Paris: Presses Universitaires de France.

Guerlac, H. (1983), 'Theological Voluntarism and Biological Analogies in Newton's Physical Thought', *Journal of the History of Ideas*, XLIV, pp. 549 ff.

Habermas, J. (1990), *Vergangenheit als Zukunft*, Zürich: Pendo Verlag.

Habermas, J. (1992), *Faktizität und Geltung. Beiträge zur Diskurstheorie des Rechts und des demokratischen Rechtsstaates*, Frankfurt a.M.: Suhrkamp. Translated by W. Rehg as *Between Facts and Norms: Contribution to a Discourse Theory of Law and Democracy* (1996), Cambridge, MA: MIT Press.

Habermas, J. (1996), *Die Einbeziehung des Anderen. Studien zur politischen Theorie*, Frankfurt a.M.: Suhrkamp.

Habermas, J. (1998), *Zur Legitimation durch Menschenrechte*, in J. Habermas, *Die postnationale Konstellation*, Frankfurt a.M.: Suhrkamp.

Hauriou, M. (1923), *Précis de droit constitutionnel*, Paris: Sirey.

Heidegger, M. (1950), *Holzwege*, Frankfurt a.M.: Vittorio Klostermann.

Heidegger, M. (1957), *Der Satz vom Grund*, Pfullingen: Neske.

Hissette, R. (1977), *Enquête sur les 219 articles condamnés à Paris le 7 mars 1277*, Louvain: Publications Universitaires – Paris: Vander-Oyez.

Holub, J. (1950), 'Ordinaria potentia – absoluta potentia', *Revue historique de droit français et étranger*, pp. 92 ff.

Horkheimer, M. (1938), 'Montaigne und die Funktion der Skepsis', *Zeitschrift für Sozialforschung*, 7. Translated by G. F. Hunter et al. as 'Montaigne and the Function of Skepticism', in M. Horkheimer, *Between Philosophy and Social Science: Selected Early Writings* (1993), Cambridge, MA: MIT Press.

Jalabert, J. (1960), *Le Dieu de Leibniz*, Paris: Presses Universitaires de France.

Kantorowicz, E. H. (1957), *The King's Two Bodies: A Study in Mediaeval Political Theology*, Princeton: Princeton University Press.

Kelsen, H. (1922–3), 'Gott und Staat', *Logos. Internationale Zeitschrift für Philosophie der Kultur*, vol. 11, pp. 261 ff.

Kelsen, H. (1944), *Peace through Law*, Chapel Hill: University of North Carolina Press.

Kodalle, K. M. (1973), *Politik als Macht und Mythos. Carl Schmitts 'Politische Theologie'*, Stuttgart-Berlin: Kohlhammer.

Koselleck, R. (1959), *Kritik und Krise. Ein Beitrag zur Pathogenese der bürgerlichen Welt*, Freiburg-München: Alber.

Kriele, M. (1981), *Einführung in die Staatslehre*, Opladen: Westdeutscher Verlag.

Krockow (Graf von), Chr. (1958), *Die Entscheidung. Eine Untersuchung über Ernst Jünger, Carl Schmitt, Martin Heidegger*, Stuttgart: Enke.

Landucci, S. (1992), 'Sulle "verità eterne" in Spinoza', in D. Bostrenghi (ed.), *Hobbes e Spinoza: Atti del Convegno internazionale di Urbino*, 14–17 ottobre 1988, Naples: Bibliopolis, pp. 23 ff.

Leff, G. (1975), *William of Ockham. The Metamorphosis of Scholastic Discourses*, Manchester: Manchester University Press.

Lenoble (S. J.), R. (1943), *Mersenne, ou la naissance du mécanisme*, Paris: Vrin.

Lombardi Vallauri, L. (1999), *Dio o Logos? La grande visione d'insieme alla prova*, in L. Lombardi Vallauri (ed.), *Logos dell'Essere – Logos della norma*, Bari: Adriatica.

Lottieri, C. (1993), 'Sul declino dell'obbligazione politica', *Biblioteca della libertà*, 122, pp. 27 ff.

Löwith, K. (1960), 'Der okkasionelle Dezisionismus von C. Schmitt', in K. Löwith, *Gesammelte Abhandlungen. Zur Kritik der geschichtlichen Existenz*, Stuttgart: Kohlhammer.

Lübbe, H. (1994), *Abschied vom Superstaat*, Berlin: Siedler.

Luciani, M. (1995), 'Quattordici argomenti contro l'invocazione del potere costituente', *Democrazia e diritto*, vol. 35, n. 3–4, pp. 97 ff.

Luciani, M. (1996), 'L'antisovrano e la crisi delle costituzioni', *Rivista di diritto costituzionale*, 1.

Luhmann, N. (1969), *Legitimation durch Verfahren*, Neuwied: Luchterhand.

Marini, G. (1998), *Tre studi sul cosmopolitismo kantiano*, Pisa and Rome: Istituti Editoriali e Poligrafici Internazionali.

Marrone, J. (1974), 'The Absolute and the Ordained Powers of the Pope. An Unedited Text of Henry of Ghent', *Medieval Studies*, XXXV, pp. 7 ff.

Marx, K. [1858] (1956), 'Grundrisse der Kritik der politischen Ökonomie', in *Marx-Engels-Werkausgabe*, vol. 42, Berlin: Dietz.

Marxen, A. (1937), *Das Problem der Analogie zwischen den Seinsstrukturen der grossen Gemeinschaften. Dargestellt im engeren Anschluß an die Schriften von Carl Schmitt und Eric Peterson*, Würzburg: Konrad Triltsch Verlag.

McIlwain, C. H. (1940), *Constitutionalism. Ancient and Modern*, Ithaca, NY: Cornell University Press.

Miethke, J. (1969), *Ockhams Weg zur Sozialphilosophie*, Berlin: De Gruyter.

Miglio, G. (1993), 'Introduzione' to H. D. Thoreau, *Disobbedienza civile*, Milan: Mondadori.

Mollat, G. (1885), *Rechtsphilosophisches aus Leibnitzens ungedruckten Schriften*, ed. G. Mollat, Leipzig: J. H. Robolskyl.

Moonan, L. (1974), 'St. Thomas Aquinas on Divine Power', *Atti del Convegno internazionale per il VII centenario di*

Tommaso d'Aquino, Rome and Naples: Città Nuova, pp. 366 ff.

Muckle, J. T. (1933), *Algazel's Metaphysics. A Medieval Translation*, ed. J. T. Muckle, Toronto: St Michael's College.

(de) Muralt, A. (1966), 'Epoché – Malin Génie – Théologie de la toute-puissance divine. Le concept objectif sans objet: recherche d'une structure de pensée', *Studia philosophica*, XXVI, pp. 159 ff.

(de) Muralt, A. (1978), 'La structure de la philosophie politique moderne. D'Occam à Rousseau', in *Souveraineté et pouvoir*, Génève, Lausanne and Neuchâtel: *Cahiers de la Revue de Théologie et de Philosophie*, pp. 3 ff.

Negri, A. (1970), *Descartes politico, o della ragionevole ideologia*, Milan: Feltrinelli.

Negri, A. (1982), *L'anomalia selvaggia. Saggio su potere e potenza in Baruch Spinoza*, Milan: Feltrinelli.

Negri, A. (1992), *Il potere costituente. Saggio sulle alternative del moderno*, Milan: SugarCo.

Oakley, F. (1961), 'Medieval Theories of Natural Law: William of Ockham and the Significancy of the Voluntarist Tradition', *Natural Law Forum*, 6, pp. 65 ff.

Oakley, F. (1968), 'Jacobean Political Theology: The Absolute and Ordinary Powers of the King', *Journal of the History of Ideas*, XXIX, pp. 323 ff.

Oakley, F. (1984), *Omnipotence, Covenant and Order. An Exercise in the History of Ideas from Abelard to Leibniz*, Ithaca and London: Cornell University Press.

Oberman, H. A. (1975), 'The Shape of Late Medieval Thought: the Birth Pangs of the Modern Era', in H. A. Oberman and Ch. Trinkhaus (eds), *The Pursuit of Holiness in the Late Medieval and Renaissance Religion*, Leiden: E. J. Brill, pp. 3 ff.

Onfray, M. (1997), *Politique du rebelle. Traité de résistance et d'insoumission*, Paris: Grasset.

Osler, M. J. (1985), 'Eternal Truths and the Laws of Nature: the Theological Foundations of Descartes' Philosophy of Nature', *Journal of the History of Ideas*, XLVI, pp. 349 ff.

Pacchi, A. (1965), *Convenzione e ipotesi nella formazione della filosofia naturale di Thomas Hobbes*, Florence: La Nuova Italia.

Palombella, G. (1997), *Costituzione e sovranità. Il senso della democrazia costituzionale*, Bari: Dedalo.

Pasqualucci, P. (1978), 'Felicità messianica. Interpretazione del Frammento teologico-politico di Benjamin', *Rivista internazionale di filosofia del diritto*, LV, 3, pp. 583 ff.

Passerin d'Entrèves, A. (1962), *La dottrina dello Stato. Elementi di analisi e di interpretazione*, Turin: Giappichelli.

Pernoud, M. A. (1970), 'Innovation in Ockham's References to the "potentia Dei"', *Antonianum*, XLV, pp. 65 ff.

Pernoud, M. A. (1972), 'The Theory of the "potentia Dei" according to Aquinas, Scotus and Ockham', *Antonianum*, XLVII, pp. 395 ff.

Pintard, R. (1943), *Le libertinage érudit dans la première moitié du XVIIe siècle*, Paris: Boivin.

Popkin, R. H. (1968), *The History of Scepticism from Erasmus to Descartes*, New York: Humanities Press.

Portinaro, P. P. (1993), *La rondine, il topo e il castoro. Apologia del realismo politico*, Venice: Marsilio.

Quaritsch, H., ed. (1988), *Complexio Oppositorum. Über Carl Schmitt*, Berlin: Duncker & Humblot.

Randi, E. (1986a), *Il sovrano e l'orologiaio. Due immagini di Dio nel dibattito sulla 'potentia absoluta' fra XIII e XIV secolo*, Florence: La Nuova Italia.

Randi, E. (1986b), 'Lex est in potestate agentis. Note per una storia dell'idea scotista di "potentia absoluta"', in M. T. Beonio-Brocchieri Fumagalli (ed.), *Sopra la volta del mondo. Onnipotenza e potenza assoluta di Dio tra Medioevo ed età moderna*, Bergamo: Lubrina, pp. 129 ff.

Riley, P. (1986), *The General Will before Rousseau*, Princeton: Princeton University Press.

Roehrssen, C. (1980), 'Critiche della destra weimariana a Kelsen. Risvolti culturali del contrastato ingresso del mondo borghese nell'ambito culturale tedesco', *Materiali per una storia della cultura giuridica*, 2, pp. 471 ff.

Rosso, C. (1954), *Moralisti del 'bonheur'*, Turin: Edizioni di Filosofia.

Ruini, C. (1980), 'La nuova "teologia politica" tedesca', *Il Mulino*, 6, pp. 894 ff.

Rumpf, M. (1976), *Radikale Theologie. Benjamins Beziehung zu Carl Schmitt*, in *Walter Benjamin. Zeitgenosse der Moderne*, Kronberg: Scriptor.

Sauerwein, H. (1960), *Die Omnipotenz des 'pouvoir constituant'. Ein Beitrag zur Staats- und Verfassungstheorie*, Diss. Rechtswiss. Fakultät der J.-W., Frankfurt a.m.: Goethe Universität.

Schmitt, C. (1921; 1928²), *Die Diktatur. Von den Anfängen des modernen Souveränitätsgedakens bis zum proletarischen Klassenkampf*, München-Leipzig: Duncker & Humblot.

Schmitt, C. (1922), *Politische Theologie. Vier Kapitel zur Lehre von der Souveränität*, München-Leipzig: Duncker & Humblot.

Schmitt, C. (1926), *Die geistesgeschichtliche Lage des heutigen Parlamentarismus*, München-Leipzig: Duncker & Humblot.

Schmitt, C. (1928), *Verfassungslehre*, München-Leipzig: Duncker & Humblot.

Schmitt, C. (1934), *Über die drei Arten des rechtswissenschaftlichen Denkens*, Hamburg: Hanseatische Verlagsanstalt.

Schmitt, C. (1938), *Der Leviathan in der Staatslehre des Thomas Hobbes. Sinn und Fehlschlag eines politischen Symbols*, Hamburg: Hanseatische Verlagsanstalt.

Schmitt, C. (1950), *Der Nomos der Erde im Völkerrecht des Jus Publicum Europaeum*, Köln: Greven Verlag.

Schmitt, C. (1956), *Hamlet oder Hekuba. Der Einbruch der Zeit in das Spiel*, Düsseldorf-Köln: Eugen Diederichs Verlag.

Schmitt, C. (1958), *Verfassungsrechtliche Aufsätze aus den Jahren 1924–1954*, Berlin: Duncker & Humblot.

Schmitt, C. (1963a), *Der Begriff des Politischen*, Berlin: Duncker & Humblot.

Schmitt, C. (1963b), *Theorie des Partisanen*, Berlin: Duncker & Humblot.

Schmitt, C. (1965), 'Die vollendete Reformation. Bemerkungen und Hinweise zu neuen Leviathan-Interpretationen', *Der Staat*, vol. 4, n. 1, pp. 51–69.

Schmitt, C. (1967), *Die Tyrannei der Werte*, in *Säkularisation und Utopie – Ebracher Studien. Ernst Forsthoff zum 65. Geburtstag*, Stuttgart, Berlin, Köln and Mainz: Kohlhammer, pp. 37–62.

Schmitt, C. (1970), *Politische Theologie II. Die Legende der Erledigung jeder politischen Theologie*, Berlin: Duncker & Humblot.

Schmitt, C. (1991), *Glossarium. Aufzeichnungen der Jahre 1947–1951*, Berlin: Duncker & Humblot.

Schneider, G. (1970), *Der Libertin. Zur Geistes- und Sozialgeschichte des Bürgertums im 16. und 17. Jahrhundert*, Stuttgart: Metzler.

Schnur, R. (1963), *Individualismus und Absolutismus. Zur politischen Theorie vor Thomas Hobbes 1600–1640*, Berlin: Duncker & Humblot.

Schütz, A. (2012), 'Legal Modernity and Medieval Theology: the case of Duns Scotus, Ordinatio I, diss. 44', in: *The Theology of 'Potentia Dei' and the History of European Normativity*, eds A. Schütz and M. Traversino, *Divus Thomas*, spec. edn, n. 115, pp. 418 ff.

Sedlmayr, H. (1948), *Verlust der Mitte. Die bildende Kunst des 19. und 20. Jahrhunderts als Symptom und Symbol der Zeit*, Salzburg-Wien: Otto Müller.

Shute, S., and S. Hurley (1993), *Human Rights – Oxford Amnesty Lectures 1993*, New York: Basic Books.

Spitzer., L. (1963), *Classical and Christian Ideas of World Harmony*, Baltimore: The Johns Hopkins University Press.

Staff, I. (1981), 'Zum Begriff der Politischen Theologie bei Carl Schmitt', in L. Lombardi Vallauri and G. Dilcher (eds), *Cristianesimo, secolarizzazione e diritto moderno*, Milan: Giuffrè and Baden-Baden: Nomos Verlag.

Steiner, U. (1966), *Verfassunggebung und verfassunggebende Gewalt des Volkes*, Berlin: Duncker & Humblot.

Stratenwerth, G. (1951), *Die Naturrechtslehre des Johannes Duns Scotus*, Göttingen: Vandenhoeck und Ruprecht.

Strauss, L. (1952), *Persecution and the Art of Writing*, Glencoe, IL: The Free Press.

Strauss, L., and J. Cropsey, eds (1987), *History of Political Philosophy*, 3rd edition, Chicago and London: University of Chicago Press.

Taubes, J. (1983), *Religionstheorie und politische Theologie*, vol.

I: *Der Fürst dieser Welt. Carl Schmitt und die Folgen*, ed. J. Taubes, München, Paderborn, Wien and Zürich: Wilhelm Fink Verlag.

Taubes, J. (1993), *Die politische Theologie des Paulus*, München: Wilhelm Fink Verlag.

Tierney, B., and P. Linehan (1980), *Authority and Power. Studies on Medieval Law and Government presented to Walter Ullmann on his Seventieth Birthday*, Cambridge: Cambridge University Press.

Tierno Galván, E. [1951] (1971), *Los supuestos escotistas de la teoría politica de Jean Bodin*, in E. Tierno Galván, *Escritos 1950–1960*, Madrid: Tecnos.

Tommissen, P. (1975), 'Carl Schmitt e il "renouveau" cattolico nella Germania degli anni venti', *Storia e politica*, XIV, 4, pp. 481 ff.

Türcke, C. (1992), *Gewalt und Tabu. Philosophische Grundzüge*, Lüneburg: zu Klampen.

Vignaux, P. (1931), sub vocibus 'Nominalisme' and 'Occam', *Dictionnaire de Théologie Catholique*, t. XI/1, Paris: Letouzey et Ané, col. 717 ff., col. 864 ff.

Vignaux, P. (1948), *Nominalisme au XIVe siècle*, Paris: Vrin.

Villey, M. (1975), *La formation de la pensée juridique moderne*, Paris: Presses Universitaires de France.

Voegelin, E. (1931), 'Die Verfassungslehre von Carl Schmitt. Versuch einer konstruktiven Analyse ihrer staatstheoretischen Prinzipien', *Zeitschrift für öffentliches Recht*, II, p. 89 ff.

Voegelin, E. (1952), *The New Science of Politics*, Chicago: University of Chicago Press.

Walther, M. (1993), 'Carl Schmitt et Baruch Spinoza, ou les aventures du concept du politique', in O. Bloch (ed.), *Spinoza au XXe siècle*, Paris: Presses Universitaires de France.

Welzel, H. (1962), *Naturrecht und materiale Gerechtigkeit*, Göttingen: Vandenhoeck und Ruprecht.

Zweig, E. (1909), *Die Lehre vom pouvoir constituant. Ein Beitrag zum Staatsrecht der französischen Revolution*, Tübingen: J. C. B. Mohr.

Index

Index

Index